HOW TO USE THIS BOOK

Your Collins Traveller Guide will help you find your way around your holiday destination quickly and easily. It is split into two sections which are colour-coded:

The blue section provides you with an alphabetical sequence of headings, from **ART GALLERIES** to **WALKS** via **EXCURSIONS**, **RESTAURANTS**, **SHOPPING** etc. Each entry within a topic includes information on how to get there, how much it will cost you, when it will be open and what to expect. Furthermore, every page has its own map showing the position of each item and the nearest landmark. This allows you to orientate yourself quickly and easily in your new surroundings.

To find what you want to do – having dinner, visiting a museum, going for a walk or shopping for gifts – simply flick through the blue headings and take your pick!

The red section is an alphabetical list of information providing essential facts about places and cultural items – 'What is the Riesenrad?', 'When is the Vienna International Music Festival?', 'Where is Grinzing?' – and expanding on subjects touched on in the first half of the book. This section also contains practical travel information. It ranges through how to find accommodation, where to hire a car, the variety of eating places and food available, tips on health, information on money, which newspapers are available, how to find a taxi and where the youth hostels are. It is lively and informative and easy to use. Each band shows the first three letters of the first entry on the page. Simply flick through the bands till you find the entry you need!

All the main entries are also cross-referenced to help you find them. Names in small capitals – **CHILDREN** – tell you that there is more information about the item you are looking for under the topic on children in the first part of the book. So when you read 'see **CHILDREN**' you turn to the blue heading for **CHILDREN**. The instruction 'see **A-Z**' after a word lets you know that the word has its own entry in the second part of the book. Similarly words in bold type – **Hofburg** – also let you know that there is an entry in the A-Z for the indicated name. In both cases you just look under the appropriate heading in the red section.

Packed full of information and easy to use – you'll always know where you are with your Collins Traveller Guide!

Vienna

HarperCollins*Publishers*

This book was produced using QuarkXPress™ and
Adobe Illustrator 88™ on Apple Macintosh™ computers
and output to separated film on a Linotronic™ 300 Imagesetter

Text: Callum Brines
Photography: T. F. Larsen-Collinge ABIPP
Cartography: Susan Harvey Design
Design: Ted Carden

First published 1991
Copyright © HarperCollins Publishers
Produced by Collins Manufacturing, Glasgow
ISBN 0 00 435753-1

The very name of Vienna, the Austrian capital, conjures up an image of elegance, music, grandeur and grace. This is the city of the Strauss family, who filled it with the melodic strains of the waltz, where Mozart, Brahms, Liszt, Schubert, Bach, Beethoven and Mahler all took up residence at one time or another in their careers in order to compose in the atmosphere most conducive to their geniuses. With them came the balls, opera houses and concert halls where a carefree, gay Vienna danced to, and was moved and entertained by some of the loveliest music the world has ever heard. You can still appreciate this legacy of Europe's most musical city in the present-day cultural calendar of operas, ballets, concerts, and balls (especially the annual Opera Ball held during *Fasching* or 'Carnival') at venues such as the Konzerthaus, the Opera House or the Musikverein – all redolent of the glittering days of the Hapsburg empire.

While there is no doubt that the late 18thC and the early 19thC period of the Viennese School of composers constitutes the city's musical heyday, the 'cultural capital' of Wien was also a mecca for all devotees of the arts: painters, sculptors, designers, architects and writers were all drawn by its magnetic influence, especially in the 19thC. The world-renowned Burgtheater ('Burg' for short), which was originally established in the Hofburg under the auspices of Empress Maria Theresa, moved to the beautiful pillared building which it now occupies on the Ringstrasse. The theatre attracted the world of drama's most famous names, and still does thanks to extensive rebuilding done in the early 1950s when it was restored to its former glory after near-destruction by fire at the end of World War II. Another imperial institution, the Vienna Boys' Choir (the brainchild of Emperor Maximilian I), is still one of the city's main attractions, and the beautiful tones of the boys' voices can be heard by visitors every week in the Hofburgkapelle (Court Chapel).

While the imperial family deserve all credit for fostering the arts and

culture in their imperial capital, another blossoming occurred, this time in the visual arts, in reaction to what was felt to be the restrictiveness of the official bodies of the Küstlerhaus and the Akademie der bildenden Kunst – institutions responsible for, for example, the Ringstrasse's grand and weighty buildings. This reaction was embodied in the work of the Viennese Secession led by Gustav Klimt which, at the turn of the century, gave the city its Art-Nouveau, or *Jugendstil*, face-lift, paralleling the experience of Glasgow. Indeed, Klimt was heavily influenced by Glaswegian architect and artist Charles

Schloss Schönbrunn

Rennie Mackintosh, who exhibited in Joseph Olbrich's famous Secession Building (nicknamed the Golden Cabbage due to the shape of its bronze cupola) which is inscribed with the words, 'To every age its art, to art its freedom.' Other notable Art-Nouveau buildings from this period to look out for as you explore the city are Otto Wagner's Stadtbahn and Kirche am Steinhof, and Adolf Loos' Steiner House. The highly distinctive and supremely decorative works of Gustav Klimt, and those of his fellow artists Egon Schiele and Oskar Kokoschka, who became two of this century's greatest expressionist artists, can be seen, along with the treasures of the imperial collections, in Vienna's remarkable public museums and galleries. Most prominent among these are the Künsthistorisches Museum (one of the best of its kind in the world), the Academy of Fine Arts, the Historical Museum of the City of Vienna, and the Academy of Applied Arts. Still more galleries and museums, such as the Baroque Museum, the Imperial Apartments, the Imperial Coach Collection, the Army Museum, the Österreichische Galerie and the Treasury, are housed in Vienna's royal palaces of Belvedere, Schloss Schönbrunn and the Hofburg – none of which should be missed. The first was built for Prince Eugene of Savoy and consists of two buildings beautifully sited on a slope overlooking the city. The second, the Hapsburgs' magnificent summer residence on the outskirts of the city, was built by Empress Maria Theresa and modelled on the French palace of Versailles. It boasts lavish formal gardens and an ornamental hill-top temple. The Hofburg, the family's more modest yet still massive winter residence in the Innere Stadt, stands near the Spanish Riding School where you can still watch the famous Lippizaner horses being put through their paces.

The Innere Stadt itself is the oldest and loveliest part of this beautiful city on the not-so-blue (as every visitor to the city has noted) Danube. The historical centre is encircled by the three-kilometre-long Ringstrasse which was built on the original fortifications surrounding the city, and which contains most of Vienna's finest buildings (and shops): the University (noted for its medical school), the Rathaus (City Hall), the Votivkirche, the Opera House, Parliament, the Stock Exchange and the Burgtheater, to mention just a few. Stephansplatz, almost at the heart of the district, is dominated by the medieval cathedral, Stephansdom, with its wonderful glazed-tile roof. At night there is no more delightful sight than that of the illuminated sculptures and decorations embellishing the district's ornate roofs and buildings. In sharp contrast to this are the areas less well known to the tourist, but of deep interest to social scientists and town planners, districts where the massive complexes of workers' housing were erected by the social-ist municipality which administered the city during the interwar period when the city was known as 'Red Vienna'.

It may be a relief, even to the most avid culture vulture, to discover that Vienna, this most hedonistic of cities, also offers the simpler pleasures of life in addition to its music, drama, art and architecture. Alternate an evening at the opera with a visit to a jolly *Heuriger* (inn) in one of the wine-growing suburbs (the most touristy being Grinzing), where the deceptively light, new wine is drunk prodigiously from *Viertels* (little quarter-litre mugs resembling beer mugs). As the evening progresses the atmosphere can get extremely raucous, and the rendering of folk songs extremely loud! Another informal type of establishment, a more recent development than that of the traditional *Heuriger*, is the *Beisel*, a type of pub/restaurant where you can find good, unpretentious cooking at reasonable prices and with musical accompaniment. However, if you can afford it, try at least once to sample the outstanding cuisine, setting and ambience of one of Vienna's elegant, but costly, restaurants. The most famous is the Sacher, where the Sachertorte originated, in the hotel of the same name on Philharmonikerstrasse; the most atmospher-ic is the frescoed Rathauskeller, situated, as its name suggests, in the vaulted cellars of City Hall.

As for daytime pleasures, try alternating a physically tiring day in a museum or gallery, with one spent relaxing in the city's *Kaffeehäuser* (coffee houses), where comfortable burghers read newspapers from around the world, play chess (or even bridge), converse, or read while sampling the delicious cakes and pastries for which Vienna is justly famed (indeed it is hardly possible to pass a patisserie without being drawn inside to purchase one of the mouthwatering delicacies dis-played in the window). But if this is too sedentary an occupation to keep you amused for long, then there is a choice of lovely parks in which to stroll. The Stadtpark, on the banks of the Danube, is perhaps

the most impressive of these, and contains statues of some of Vienna's famous artistic and musical personalities, the most notable being that of Johann Strauss by Edmund Hellmer. Neither should you miss the romantic Wienerwald (Vienna Woods), immortalized by Strauss's music, covering the last foothills of the Alps outside the city.

Another, more artificial, attraction is the world-famous Prater. Once an imperial deer park of some 2000 acres and the site of a the World Exhibition of 1897, it is now a huge fairground dominated by the Riesenrad, the giant Ferris wheel which is the largest in the world, built here for the exhibition. The view from the top of the slowly revolving wheel is rivalled only by the panorama offered from the viewing platform of the 252-m-high Donauturm beside the Donaupark.

There are more opportunities for leisure on the Donauinsel (Danube Island), with its miles of beaches, marinas and water-sport facilities (it can be reached easily on the underground); while another island, Wolfsau, is the location of the Augarten palace, home of the Vienna Boys' Choir and the famous Vienna Porcelain Manufactory.

Historically and geographically, Vienna has occupied a strategic position in Europe – it was here that the Congress of Vienna (1814-15) effected the settlement of Europe after the Napoleonic Wars – and acted as a bulwark against the encroachment of the Ottoman empire. Over the centuries the city managed to resist repeated Turkish attacks, but it has been occupied by other invaders: the French under Napoleon, Swedish forces during the Thirty Years' War, the Nazis in World War II, and finally the Allied forces until 1955, when it at last became free and independent. Although Vienna suffered from bomb damage during World War II, it escaped the wholesale destruction experienced in parts of many German cities, and we have to be thankful that so many fine buildings and monuments have remained intact in the home of Freud and Mozart, this centre of culture and civilization, one of the most beautiful cities in Europe and one of the most pleasurable to visit.

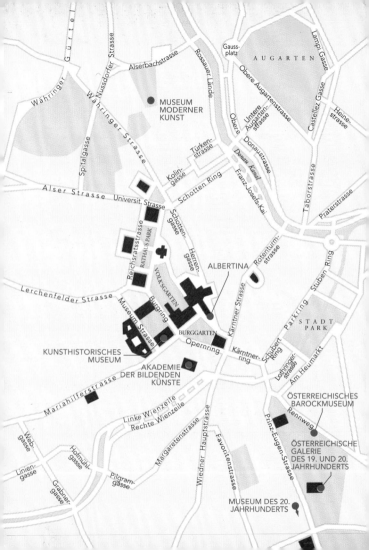

WÄHRINGER GÜRTEL

Nussdorfer Strasse

Alserbachstrasse

Rossauer Lände

Gaussplatz

AUGARTEN

Lampi Gasse

Castelliez Gasse

Obere Augartenstrasse

Heine strasse

Währinger Park

Währinger Strasse

MUSEUM MODERNER KUNST

Obere Donaustrasse

Untere Augartenstrasse

Donaustrasse

Spitalgasse

Türkenstrasse

Donau Kanal

Taborstrasse

Alser Strasse

Universit. Strasse

Kolingasse

Schotten Ring

Franz-Josefs-Kai

Praterstrasse

Reichsratsstrasse

RATHAUS PARK

Schottengasse

Herrengasse

Rotenturmstrasse

Lerchenfelder Strasse

VOLKSGARTEN

Burgring

ALBERTINA

Kärntner Strasse

Stuben Ring

STADT PARK

Parkring

Museum Strasse

BURGGARTEN

Opernring

KUNSTHISTORISCHES MUSEUM

Kärntnerring

Schubert Ring

Am Heumarkt

AKADEMIE DER BILDENDEN KÜNSTE

Mariahilferstrasse

Lehringerstrasse

ÖSTERREICHISCHES BAROCKMUSEUM

Rennweg

Linke Wienzeile

Rechte Wienzeile

Margaretenstrasse

Favoritenstrasse

Wiedner Hauptstrasse

Prinz-Eugen-Strasse

ÖSTERREICHISCHE GALERIE DES 19. UND 20. JAHRHUNDERTS

Weibgasse

Liniengasse

Hofmühlgasse

Grabnergasse

Pilgramgasse

MUSEUM DES 20. JAHRHUNDERTS

KUNSTHISTORISCHES MUSEUM Burgring 5 (Maria Theresien Platz).
❑ 1000-1600 Tue.-Fri., 0900-1600 Sat.-Sun. U Mariahilferstrasse. Bus 2A, 3A. Tram 1, 2, D, J. ❑ 30 Sch.
World-class museum housing most of the superb Hapsburg collection and featuring every major artist from the Renaissance onwards. See **A-Z**.

AKADEMIE DER BILDENDEN KÜNSTE Schillerplatz 3.
❑ 1000-1400 Tue., Wed., Fri.; 1000-1300, 1500-1800 Wed., 0900-1300 Sat.-Sun. U Karlsplatz. Bus 57A. Tram 1, 2, 52, D, J. ❑ 15 Sch.
The academy's galleries house exceptional old masters including works by Rembrandt, Rubens, Bosch and Van Dyke. See **A-Z**.

MUSEUM DES 20. JAHRHUNDERTS Schweitzergarten.
❑ 1000-1800 Thu.-Tue. U Südbahnhof. Tram D. ❑ Variable.
The Austrian Pavilion at the 1958 World Fair is now a venue for temporary exhibitions of contemporary art. Important sculpture garden.

ALBERTINA Augustinerstrasse 1.
❑ 1000-1600 Mon., Tue., Thu.; 1000-1800 Wed., 1000-1400 Fri., 1000-1300 Sat.-Sun. (closed Sun. July & Aug.). U Karlsplatz. ❑ 15 Sch.
The world's most important collection of graphic art. See **WALK 3**, **A-Z**.

MUSEUM MODERNER KUNST Fürstengasse 1.
❑ 1000-1800 Wed.-Mon. Bus 40A. Tram D. ❑ 30 Sch.
Works of 20thC artists including Klimt, Picasso, Magritte and Warhol displayed in one of Vienna's most beautiful baroque buildings. See **A-Z**.

ÖSTERREICHISCHE GALERIE DES 19. UND 20. JAHRHUNDERTS Pr.-Eugen-Str. 27.
❑ 1000-1600 Tue.-Sun. U Karlsplatz, Taubstummengasse. ❑ 30 Sch.
Austrian art of 19th-20thC housed in the Upper Belvedere. See **A-Z**.

ÖSTERREICHISCHES BAROCKMUSEUM Rennweg 6a.
❑ 1000-1600 Tue.-Sun. U Karlsplatz. ❑ 30 Sch.
A collection of Austrian baroque art. See **Belvedere-Schlösser**.

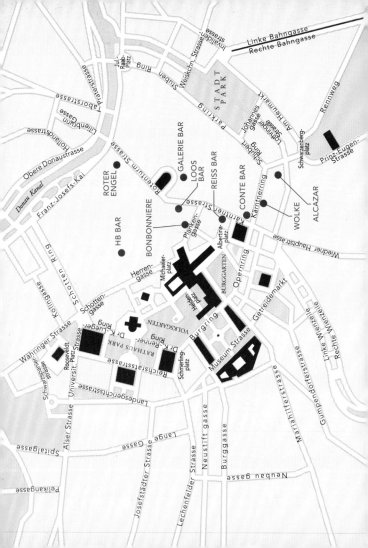

ALCAZAR Bösendorferstrasse 2.
❑ 0900-1300 Mon.-Sat., 1900-0200 Sun. U Karlsplatz. Tram 1, 2.
A very popular cocktail bar with a varied clientele.

BONBONNIERE Spiegelgasse 15.
❑ 1500-0200 Mon.-Sat. U Stephansplatz.
Plush, turn-of-the-century decor. Winter garden and live piano music.

CONTE BAR Kärntnerring 3.
❑ 1700-0400 Mon.-Sat. U Karlsplatz.
Fashionable after-dinner/theatre meeting place.

HB BAR Naglergasse 5.
❑ 1600-0200 Mon.-Sat. U Stephansplatz.
Pleasant bar, especially in summer on the terrace.

LOOS BAR Kärntner Strasse 10.
❑ 1800-0400. U Stephansplatz.
Designed by Adolf Loos. Recently reopened after extensive renovation.

ROTER ENGEL Raben Steig 5.
❑ 1500-0400 Mon.-Sat., 1500-0200 Sun. U Schwedenplatz. Tram 1, 2.
Frequented by a young and trendy clientele enjoying the good wine and music (often live).

REISS BAR Marco d'Avianog 1.
❑ 1100-0300 Sun.-Fri., 1000-0300 Sat. U Stephansplatz.
Ideal location for a rendezvous before or after an evening out.

GALERIE BAR Singerstrasse 7.
❑ 1800-0400 Mon.-Fri., 1900-0400 Sat.-Sun. U Stephansplatz.
The popular gallery overlooks the hubbub below.

WOLKE Kärntnerring 10.
❑ 2000-0500. On corner of Akademiestrasse. U Karlsplatz. Tram 1, 2.
Modern, stylish bar, popular with the city's avant-garde.

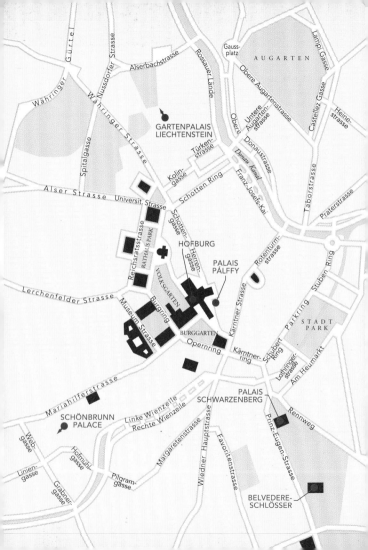

Palaces

HOFBURG Michaelerplatz 1.
❑ Tour in English of Imperial apartments 0830-1630 (Sun. & hol. until 1300). U Stephansplatz/Mariahilferstrasse. ❑ 30 Sch.
From its origins as a 13thC medieval castle, the building has evolved through the centuries into the marvellous city within a city that it is today. See WALK 3, A-Z.

SCHÖNBRUNN PALACE Schönbrunner Schlossstrasse.
❑ State apartments 0900-1200, 1300-1700 May-Sep. (Oct.-April until 1700). U Schönbrunn/Heitzing. Bus 15A. Tram 10, 58.
Magnificent baroque summer residence of the Hapsburgs, surrounded by a beautiful park. See A-Z.

BELVEDERE-SCHLÖSSER Rennweg 6, Prinz-Eugen-Strasse 27.
❑ 1000-1600 Tue.,Thu., Sat.; 1000-1300 Fri., 0900-1200 Sun. (Son et lumière at 2130 in summer). U Karlsplatz/Taubstummengasse. Tram D.
Two baroque palaces, originally built for Prince Eugene, now house three museums of the Austrian Gallery. See ART GALLERIES, A-Z.

PALAIS SCHWARZENBERG Rennweg 2.
U Karlsplatz. Bus 4A. Tram D, 71.
This palace was originally one of the first summer residences built outside the city walls. It has a fine interior (now partly a hotel) and magnificent baroque gardens.

PALAIS PÁLFFY Josephsplatz 6.
U Stephansplatz. Bus 2A.
Converted into a nobleman's residence at the end of the 16thC. Mozart first produced his Figaro here in a room now called the Figarosaal.

GARTENPALAIS LIECHTENSTEIN Fürstengasse 1.
Bus 40A. Tram D.
An attractive 17thC building with frescoes depicting the story of Hercules. It is also the home of the Museum Moderner Kunst (see ART GALLERIES, A-Z).

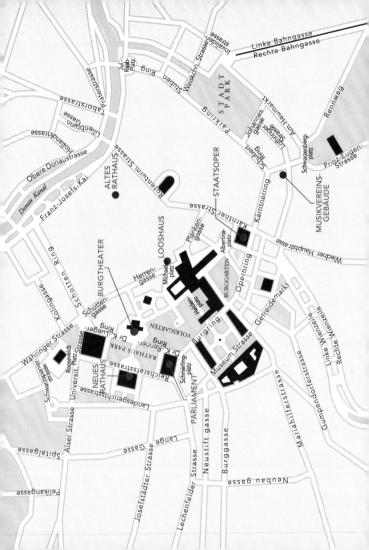

STAATSOPER Opernring 2.
U Karlsplatz. Tram 1, 2, D, J.
Built between 1861 and 1869, Vienna's magnificent Opera House is among the world's three greatest. See **WALK 3**, **A-Z**.

ALTES RATHAUS Wipplingerstrasse 6-8.
U Stephansplatz. Bus 1A, 2A, 3A.
Under municipal ownership since 1316, the Old Town Hall has undergone numerous changes and boasts a beautiful and delicate facade. The Andromeda Fountain in the courtyard is the work of Raphael Donner.

PARLIAMENT Dr Karl-Renner-Ring 3.
❏ Tours 1100 Mon.-Fri. (1000, 1300, 1400 July, Aug.).
U Lerchenfelderstrasse. Bus 48A. Tram 1, 2, D, J.
Built 1873-83 for the Imperial and Provincial Delegations and, since 1918, meeting place of the National and Federal Parliament. See **WALK 2**.

BURGTHEATER Dr Karl-Lueger-Ring 2.
❏ Tours 0900, 1100, 1300, 1400, 1500 Mon.-Fri.
U Rathaus/Schottentor. Tram 1, 2, D.
Originally dating from 1888, the theatre was rebuilt after a fire in 1945, and the French-style baroque interior lavishly restored. See **WALK 2**.

MUSIKVEREINSGEBÄUDE Dumbastrasse 3.
U Karlspaltz. Bus 4A, 59A. Tram 1, 2, D, J.
Home of the famous Golden Hall where the Vienna Philharmonic Orchestra gives its major concerts. See **A-Z**.

LOOSHAUS Michaelerplatz 5.
Designed by Adolph Loos in 1910-11, in reaction to the prevailing Art-Nouveau style, and recently renovated. See **WALK 3**.

NEUES RATHAUS Rathausplatz.
U Rathaus.
The present Town Hall dates from 1782-1884 and was designed in neo-Gothic style by Friedrich von Schmidt. See **WALK 2**.

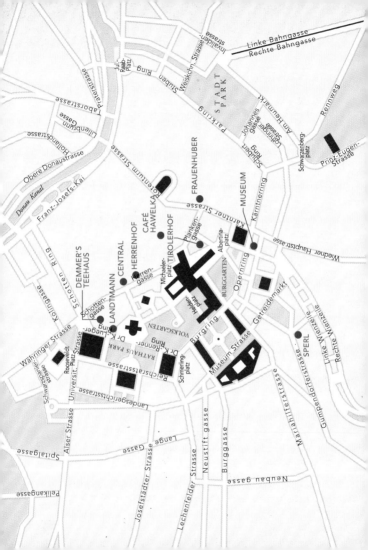

CAFÉS

CAFÉ HAWELKA Dorotheergasse 6.
❏ 0800-0200 Wed.-Mon., 1600-0200 Sun. U Stephansplatz.
Authentic Middle-European café and meeting place of Vienna's art world. Fresh Buchtel (jam-filled dumplings) at 2300 every evening.

FRAUENHUBER Himmelfortgasse 6.
❏ 0800-2200 Mon.-Fri., 0800-1500 Sat. U Stephansplatz.
The oldest and most atmospheric coffee house in Vienna.

CENTRAL Herrengasse 14.
❏ 1000-2200 Mon.-Sat. U Schottentor. Bus 1A.
Recently restored to its original Art-Nouveau glory. Live piano music.

TIROLERHOF Tegetthoffstrasse 8.
❏ 0700-2100 Mon.-Sat., 0930-2000 Sun. & hol. U Karlsplatz.
*Typical coffee house, ideal for a break after visiting Albertina (see **A-Z**).*

SPERL Gumpendorferstrasse 11.
❏ 0700-2300 Mon.-Sat., 1500-2300 Sun. U Mariahilferstr. Bus 57A.
This is the café for you if you are a billiards fan.

MUSEUM Friedrichstrasse 6.
❏ 0700-2300. U Karlsplatz.
Interior design by Adolph Loos. Large selection of international papers.

LANDTMANN Dr Karl-Lueger-Ring 4.
❏ 0800-2400. Next to Burgtheater. U Schottentor. Bus 1, 2.
Large terrace attracts a distinguished clientele of artists, politicians, etc.

HERRENHOF Herrengasse 10.
❏ 0700-2200 Mon.-Fri., 0900-2200 Sat. U Schottentor. Bus 1A.
One of Vienna's largest and loveliest coffee houses. Champagne bar.

DEMMER'S TEEHAUS Mölkerbastei 5.
❏ 0900-1800 Mon.-Fri., 0900-1200 Sat. U Schottentor. Tram 1, 2.
Top spot for a good cup of tea! Also English sandwiches, toast and cakes.

BOAT TRIPS DDSG

Wagramer Strasse

Alte Donau

A22

Neue Donau

Reichsbrücke

Donau

Handelskai

DONAUINSEL

A22

Handelskai

VOLKSPRATER

Haupallee

A23

Shüttelstrasse

Erdberger Lände

Donau Kanal

PLANETARIUM

Rennweg

Obere Donaustrasse

SPANISH RIDING SCHOOL

ZIRKUS- UND CLOWNMUSEUM

Gürtel

Gentzgasse

Währinger Strasse

HAUS DES MEERES

Burggasse

Linke Wienzeile

Gürtel

Gürtel

Hernalser Hauptstrasse

Gablenzgasse

Felberstrasse

Wien Fluss

Eichenstrasse

Edelsinnstrasse

Grünbergstrasse

STREETCAR MUSEUM

Flötzersteig

Hadikgasse

Linzer Strasse

TIERGARTEN SCHÖNBRUNN

Maxingstrasse

HAUS DES MEERES Esterházypark.
❏ 0900-1800. Bus 57A.
Housed in a World War II anti-aircraft flak tower is an interesting assortment of 3000 fish and reptiles.

TIERGARTEN SCHÖNBRUNN Schönbrunner Schlossstrasse.
❏ 0900-1700. Access is through the castle, to the right of the gardens.
U Schönbrunn. Tram 10, 58. Bus 15A. ❏ 35 Sch, child 10 Sch.
Europe's oldest zoo, housed in an Imperial menagerie built in 1752.

SPANISH RIDING SCHOOL Reitschulgasse 2.
❏ 1045 Sun. (Mar.-Dec.), 1900 Wed. (April-Oct.), 0900 Sat. (shortened). Closed July, Aug. and Dec.-Mar. U Stephansplatz/Schottentor.
*Unique and exquisite performance by Lippizaner horses to music by Mozart (see **A-Z**). Reservations essential. See **A-Z**.*

ZIRKUS- UND CLOWNMUSEUM Karmelitergasse 9.
❏ 1730-1900 Wed., 1430-1700 Sat., 0900-1200 Sun. Tram 21, N.
Museum tracing the development of the circus in Austria.

VOLKSPRATER Prater.
U Praterstern. Bus 80A. Tram 1, N, O.
A large funfair with rides, shooting galleries, etc. for all ages.

STREETCAR MUSEUM Montleartstrasse 24.
❏ 0900-1700 Mon.-Fri., 1000-1200 Sun. Closed Oct.-April.
Tram 46, 48a.
An attractive collection of old Viennese trams.

PLANETARIUM Prater Hauptallee.
❏ 1500 & 1700 Sat.-Sun. for groups. U Praterstern.
Special demonstrations for children on Sundays at 0930.

BOAT TRIPS DDSG Donaureisen, Handelskai 265.
Bus 10A, 11A. Tram 21. Dep. from Reichsbrücke or nr Schwedenplatz.
*Trips along the Danube (see **A-Z**), a favourite with children.*

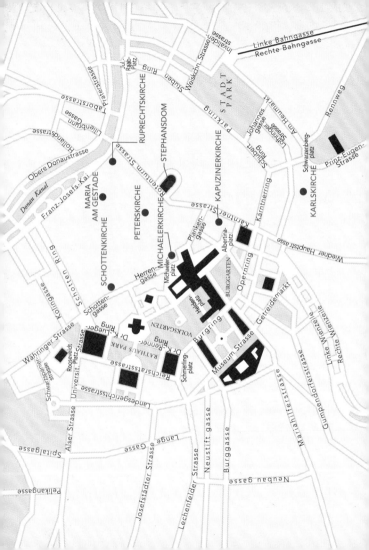

Linke Bahngasse
Rechte Bahngasse
Invalidenstrasse
Jul. Raab-Platz
Weiskirchn. Strasse
STADT PARK
Parking
Rennweg
Am Heumarkt
Praterkasse
Lilienbrunn Gasse
Taborstrasse
Hollandstrasse
RUPRECHTKIRCHE
Stuben Ring
Schubert Ring
Lothringer Strasse
Johannes Gasse
Schwarzenberg platz
Prinz-Eugen-Strasse
Obere Donaustrasse
Donau Kanal
Franz-Josefs-Kai
MARIA AM GESTADE
ROTenturm Strasse
STEPHANSDOM
KAPUZINERKIRCHE
KARLSKIRCHE
PETERSKIRCHE
SCHOTTENKIRCHE
MICHAELERKIRCHE
Planken-gasse
Kärntner Strasse
Kärntnerring
Albertina-platz
Wiedner Hauptstrasse
Herren-gasse
Michaeler platz
BURGGARTEN
Opernring
Schotten-gasse
Helden platz
Getreidemarkt
Schotten Ring
VOLKSGARTEN
Burgring
Museum Strasse
Währinger Strasse
Kolingasse
RATHAUS PARK
Dr. Renner Ring
Dr. Karl Lueger Ring
Reichsratstrasse
Schmerling-platz
Linke Wienzeile
Rechte Wienzeile
Schwarzspanier strasse
Roosevelt Platz
Universit. Platz
Landesgerichtstrasse
Gumpendorferstrasse
Alser Strasse
Spitalgasse
Josefstädter Strasse
Lange Gasse
Neustift gasse
Burggasse
Mariahilferstrasse
Lechenfelder Strasse
Neubau gasse
Pelikangasse

STEPHANSDOM Stephansplatz.

☐ Tours 1030 & 1500 Mon.-Sat., 1500 Sun. & hol. U Stephansplatz.
*The finest Gothic cathedral in Austria, completely restored after the war.
Great views of the city from the tower. See* **WALK 1**, **A-Z**.

KARLSKIRCHE Karlsplatz.

U Karlsplatz. Bus 59A, 4A. Tram 1, 2, D, J.
*Outstanding baroque structure by J. B. Fischer von Erlach. Commis-
sioned by Karl VI to mark the end of the plague in 1713. See* **A-Z**.

PETERSKIRCHE Petersplatz.

U Stephansplatz. Bus 1A, 2A, 3A.
Magnificent baroque church modelled on St Peter's in Rome. See **A-Z**.

MICHAELERKIRCHE Michaelerplatz.

U Stephansplatz. Bus 2A.
A mix of styles from late Romanesque to neoclassical. See **WALK 3**, **A-Z**.

MARIA AM GESTADE Salvatorgasse 12.

U Schwedenplatz. Bus 3A.
*Founded in 1158, rebuilt 1394-1414 and restored in the 19thC. Features
a magnificent Gothic tower. See* **WALK 2**, **A-Z**.

RUPRECHTSKIRCHE Ruprechtsplatz.

U Schwedenplatz. Tram 1, 2.
*This is the city's oldest church and it features Vienna's oldest examples
of stained glass. See* **WALK 1**, **A-Z**.

SCHOTTENKIRCHE Freyung.

U Schottentor. Bus 1A.
*Founded in the 12thC by Irish Benedictine monks. Don't miss the
baroque memorial designed by Fischer von Erlach. See* **WALK 2**, **A-Z**.

KAPUZINERKIRCHE Neuer Markt.

☐ Vault 0930-1600. U Stephansplatz.
Baroque church which contains the imperial burial vault. See **A-Z**.

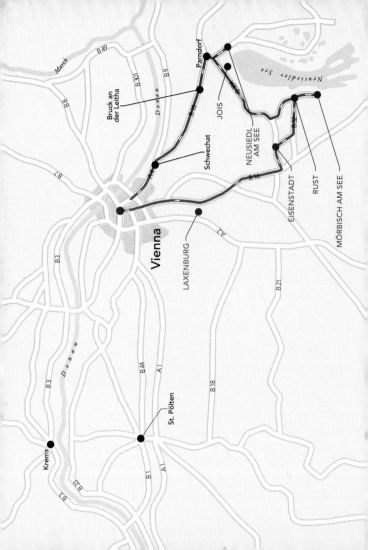

The Burgenland

162 km – *A one- or two-day round trip possibly with a stopover at Neusiedl am See. (A hotel reservation is advisable at the weekend.)*

Take route B 16 from Vienna in the direction of Eisenstadt. After 19 km turn off to the right for Laxenburg.
20 km – Laxenburg. Features various 18thC mansions and a park laid out in the English style of the late 18thC. In the middle of the lake is a mock medieval Franzensburg, built for Franz II between 1796 and 1836. Return to the B 16.

37 km – Eisenstadt (see **A-Z**). Provincial capital of the Burgenland and once the seat of the Esterházy family. The Bergkirche, just before you enter the town, is the last resting place of the composer Joseph Haydn (1732-1809). The house where he lived at Haydn 21 is now a museum and there are also rooms commemorating Liszt (0900-1200, 1300-1700 daily). He conducted his works in the Haydnsaal of the Schloss Esterházy (14thC but renovated in the 17thC), the baroque facade of which can be seen on Esterházy Platz. This room is open to the public (0800-1800) though most of the rest of the castle now houses the offices of the Burgenland administration. Continue south and take the B 52 left.

53 km – Rust. Famous for its nesting storks. There are still several 17thC houses to be seen along the main street. Visit the Fischerkirche (ask at the presbytery for the key if the church is closed) to admire the late-Gothic wooden statues of Ursula and Catherine. Turn right out of the town and head south.

59 km – Mörbisch am See. This charming village, 1.5 km from the Hungarian border, is well known for its Seebühne (stage on the lake) where operetta festivals are held each year. Turn back up to drive through Rust and continue north towards the B 304. After passing through the village of Oggau turn right onto the main road which takes you through Donneskirchen and Purbach, which are filled with beautiful old houses.

90 km – Jois. This small village offers the best views of the Neusiedler See. The reed-encircled lake is 320 km in area and is fed by subter-ranean springs. The water is lost through evaporation as it has no out-flow and in 1866 disappeared completely for 10 years. During that time it was used as farmland until it returned as suddenly as it went. On its far bank you will see the start of the Hungarian *Puszta* (Steppes). In the surrounding area one can still see old draw wells and windmills and the villages lie far apart. Some of the best Austrian wine comes from this region. On one of the smaller, shallow lakes the World Wildlife Fund has created a nature reserve which is a haven for many animals, birds and rare plants.

93 km – Neusiedl am See. Visit the 18thC Gothic parish church to admire the pulpit in the form of a boat (*Fischerkanzel*). The town is a popular weekend resort and various water sports can be practised. From here you can either continue round the lake to visit the flat marshy land to its east or head north via Parndorf (B 50), Bruck an der Leitha and Schwechat (B 10) to return to Vienna (51 km).

Schloss Esterhazy, Eisenstadt

Neusiedl am See

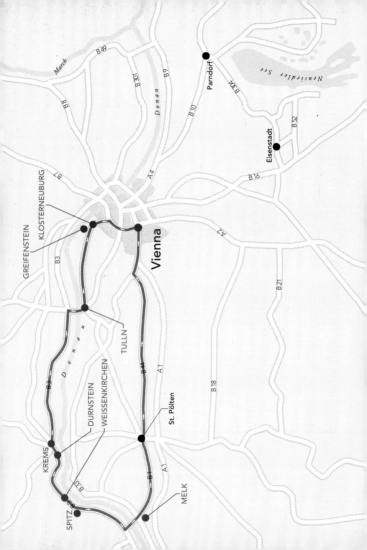

The Danube Valley

200 km – *A one- or two-day trip along the Danube to the Wachau.*

Take route B 14 northwest along the Danube
(see **A-Z**).
13 km – Klosterneuburg (see **A-Z**). The
famous 12thC Augustinian monastery of
Klosterneuburg is the largest of the many
monasteries dotted along the Danube, although
there is very little left of the original structure
which was destroyed in a fire. It is the burial
place of the patron saint of Lower Austria,
Leopold III. Leave the B 15 to the left and follow the river upstream.

21 km – Greifenstein. Just before the village,
turn left up to the 12thC castle from where you
will have a splendid view over the Danube.
The castle is open at weekends and holidays
from 1100-1800.
Continue along to rejoin the B 14. After
approximately 5 km on this road, turn right.

38 km – Tulln. This was once a river port for the Romans and was also
the meeting place of Attila, king of the Huns, and his bride, Kriemhilde.
Visit the remarkable Roman basilica, Pfarrkirche St. Stephan. Cross the
Danube and turn left onto the B 3 to head west.

72 km – Krems (see **A-Z**). Once famous for its mustard and gunpowder
and the centre of an important wine-producing region. Today it is a
beautiful, peaceful town with fine examples of Gothic, Renaissance
and baroque houses. Still on the B 3, you enter the Wachau, the name
of the part of the Danube between Krems and Melk. These 35 km cover
one of the most beautiful regions in Austria, full of vineyards and apricot orchards. You are now following a route taken by the crusaders on
their way to the Holy Land.

80 km – Durnstein. The walled village is dominated by a 12thC castle
in which Richard the Lionheart was supposedly imprisoned. According
to legend his faithful minstrel, Blondel, found him after a long search
and then returned to England to raise the ransom to free his master.

Also worth a visit is the former Augustinian monastery (now parish church) whose baroque church tower is one of the finest examples in Austria. Continue along the same route through the pretty villages of the Wachau and enjoy the wonderful views over Durnstein and the Danube.

86 km – Weissenkirchen. Visit the fortified Gothic church. There are also many fine examples of Renaissance houses. The Teisenhofer Hof houses the Museum of the Wachau (1000-1700 Tue.-Sun.).

92 km – Spitz. Here there are several examples of 16thC-18thC houses, and the Museum of the History of Navigation on the Danube, housed in Erlahof Castle (1000-1200, 1400-1600 Tue.-Sun. during summer).

97 km – Willendorf. This is where the famous *Venus*, estimated to date from 15,000-25,000 BC, was discovered. A copy is to be seen in the Naturhistorisches Museum (see MUSEUMS 2) in Vienna (the original is not on public display). Continuing along the B 3 you will see the ruins of Aggstein Castle on the far side of the river. It was once the safest stronghold along the Danube.

108 km – Melk (see **A-Z**). A pretty riverside town dominated by the famous fortified Benedictine Abbey which is well worth a visit, especially for its beautiful library (hourly guided tours 0900-1200,

Weissenkirchen

1400-1700; from 1000 Sun. & hol.).
Take the B 1 to return to Vienna (90 km) via St. Pölten, an industrial town and capital of Lower Austria.

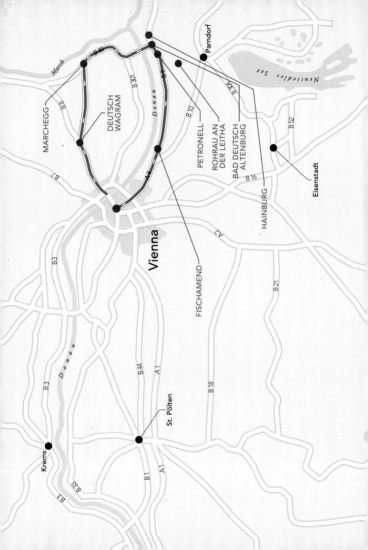

Parndorf

March

B49

MARCHEGG

B8

B7

DEUTSCH
WAGRAM

B301

Donau

B9

B10

PETRONELL

ROHRAU AN
DER LEITHA

BAD DEUTSCH
ALTENBURG

B50

Neusiedler See

B52

Eisenstadt

B16

HAINBURG

A4

Vienna

B3

FISCHAMEND

A2

B21

Donau

B44

A1

B18

B3

Donau

B3

B33

Krems

St. Pölten

B1

A1

The Marchfield

133 km – *A one-day trip to the plains north of the city.*

Take the A 4 autobahn from Vienna in the direction of Schwechat airport (16 km) where you turn off right onto the B 9.

22 km – Fischamend. Visit the Romanesque and Renaissance belfry which houses the local museum (1000-1200 Sun. May-Oct.). There are also good fish restaurants here. Follow the B 9 along the Danube.

41 km – Petronell. To the left on entering the village are the excavated remains of Roman Carnuntum, founded in AD 72. A lane leads to the Schloss Traun, home to the Donau-Museum, showing the natural history of the Danube (1000-1700 Tue.-Sun., April-mid-Nov.). Approximately 6 km south of Petronell lies the village of Rohrau an der Leitha, birthplace of Haydn (see **A-Z**). His house can be visited from 1000-1700 Tue.-Sun. There is a monument to him, erected in 1794, and you can also visit his parents' grave. A little further on is Schloss Rohrau, seat of the Harrach family, which contains the Harrach collection of paintings (1000-1700 Tue.-Sun.). Return to Petronell to pick up the B 9 again. 3 km after the village a track to the right leads to the remains of an early-2ndC AD Roman amphitheatre. Open-air plays are held here in the summer (details from the Tourist Office). Continue along the B 9.

46 km – Bad Deutsch Altenburg. A small spa town. The Museum Carnuntum houses an interesting collection of relics from the Roman occupation (1000-1700 Tue.-Sun.). The main road then runs past a bridge over the Danube to the partially walled town of Hainburg where Haydn spent his schooldays. Return to the bridge and turn right, where you cross into the Marchfeld – a rich alluvial plain known as the Battlefield of Europe. During the Napoleonic Wars the battles of Aspern and Deutsch Wagram were fought here. Continue along the B 49.

64 km – Marchegg. Situated on the River March which forms the frontier with Czechoslovakia, the Schloss here contains a large hunting museum with several rooms devoted to the flora and fauna of the region (0900-1700 April-Dec.). Climb the bastion for a view over the river and valley. From here turn left in the direction of Siebenbrunn.

90 km – Deutsch Wagram. Site of the battle of 5/6 July 1809 between the French and Austrians. There is a small museum which is worth visiting. Drive back to Vienna through the suburbs (13 km).

GIGERL Rauhensteingasse 3.
❏ 1600-0100. U Stephansplatz.
Hot and cold buffet for between 30 and 60 Sch. Good selection of local and foreign wines.

URBANI-KELLER Am Hof 12.
❏ 1800-0100 (except Sun. during June-Aug.). U Schottentor. Bus 1A.
Viennese cuisine in the cellar of a baroque house.

AUGUSTINERKELLER Augustinerstrasse 1.
❏ 1000-2400 (Sat. until 0100). U Karlsplatz. Tram 1, 2.
Live Viennese Schrammel music (two violins, a guitar and an accordion), a pretty garden and local cuisine.

ERSTERHÁZYKELLER Haarhof 1.
❏ 1000-1300, 1600-2100 Mon.-Sat., 1600-2100 Sun. U Schottentor. Bus 1A.
Hot and cold buffet with excellent wine served in one of the deepest cellars in Vienna. Not recommended if you are the least bit claustrophobic.

FIGLMÜLLER Grinzingerstrasse 55.
❏ 1700-2400 Mon.-Sat. Closed 23 Dec.-1 May. Tram 38.
This Heurige is located in a Biedermeier house.

MARTINKOVITS Bellvuestrasse 4.
❏ 1700-2400 Wed.-Fri., 1100-1500, 1700-2400 Sat.-Sun. Bus 39A.
Old Viennese Heurige/restaurant with a very pretty garden.

WEIHRAUCH Kaasgrabengasse 77.
❏ 1600-2400. Tram 38.
Popular Heurige, especially for the suckling-pig special on Thursdays.

WOLFF Rathstrasse 44-46.
❏ 1430-2400 Mon.-Sat., 1130-2400 Sun. Bus 35A.
Excellent buffet and a delightful garden.

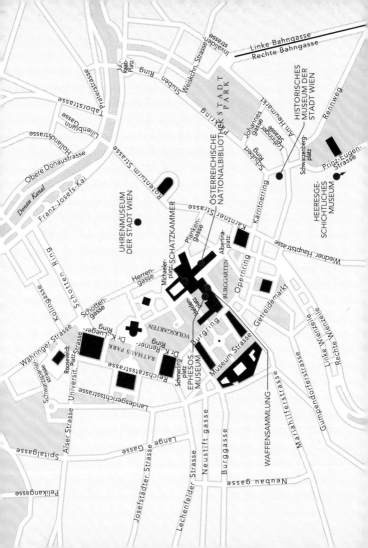

Linke Bahngasse
Rechte Bahngasse

Jul.-Raab-Platz

Invalidenstrasse

Weiskirchner Strasse

Stuben Ring

Peterstrasse

Taborstrasse

Lilienbrunngasse
Gasse

Hollandstrasse

Obere Donaustrasse

Donau Kanal

Franz-Josefs-Kai

STADT PARK

HISTORISCHES MUSEUM DER STADT WIEN

Johannesgasse

Am Heumarkt

Lothringer Strasse

Schubert Ring

Rennweg

Schwarzenbergplatz

Prinz-Eugen-Strasse

HEERESGESCHICHTLICHES MUSEUM

Rotenturm Strasse

UHRENMUSEUM DER STADT WIEN

ÖSTERREICHISCHE NATIONALBIBLIOTHEK

SCHATZKAMMER

Kärntner Strasse

Kärntnerring

Plankengasse

Albertinaplatz

Opernring

Wiedner Hauptstrasse

Herrengasse

Michaelerplatz

BURGGARTEN

Josefsplatz

Getreidemarkt

Schottengasse

Schottenring

Kolingasse

VOLKSGARTEN

Wiplinger-Platz

Burgring

Museum Strasse

Wahringer Strasse

Roosevelt

Universit. Platz

Dr.-Karl-Lueger-Strasse

Dr.-Karl-Renner-Ring

RATHAUS PARK

Schmerlingplatz

EPHESOS MUSEUM

Reichsratsstrasse

Schwarzspanierstrasse

Landesgerichtsstrasse

Alser Strasse

Lange Gasse

Reichsratsstrasse

Neustift gasse

Burggasse

WAFFENSAMMLUNG

Mariahilferstrasse

Gumpendorferstrasse

Linke Wienzeile

Rechte Wienzeile

Spitalgasse

Pelikangasse

Josefstädter Strasse

Lechenfelder Strasse

Neubau gasse

HISTORISCHES MUSEUM DER STADT WIEN Karlsplatz 8.
❏ 1000-1800 Tue.-Fri., (1900 Thu.), 1400-1700 Sat. U Karlsplatz.
Bus 4A, 59A. Tram 1, 2, 62, 65, D, J. ❏ Free.
*A fascinating and lively display chronicling the history of Vienna from
the Neolithic period to the present day. See* WALK 4, **A-Z**.

UHRENMUSEUM DER STADT WIEN Schulhof 2.
❏ 0900-1215, 1300-1630 Tue.-Sun. U Stephansplatz. Bus 1A. ❏ Free.
*Housed in the Obizzi Palace, this world-renowned collection of clocks
covers the period from 1440 to modern times.*

HEERESGESCHICHTLICHES MUSEUM Arsenalstr., Objekt 18.
❏ 1000-1600 Sat.-Thu. Bus 13A, 69A. Tram D, 18.
*Collection of military and historical relics of the Austrian Army, housed
in the oldest building in the city to have been designed as a museum.*

EPHESOS MUSEUM Heldenplatz, Neue Burg.
❏ 1000-1600 Mon., Wed.-Fri., 0900-1600 Sat.-Sun. U Mariahilferstr.
Tram 1, 2, D, J. ❏ 45 Sch.
Collection of artefacts from the ancient port on the coast of Asia Minor.

WAFFENSAMMLUNG Heldenplatz, Neue Burg.
❏ 1000-1600 Mon., Wed., Fri., 0900-1600 Sat.-Sun. U Mariahilferstr.
Tram 1, 2, D, J. ❏ 30 Sch.
Fine collection of mostly Hapsburg weapons and armour.

SCHATZKAMMER Hofburg, Schweizerhof.
❏ 1000-1600 Mon., Wed., Fri., 0900-1600 Sat.- Sun. (until 1800 April-
Oct.). U Mariahilferstrasse. Bus 2A. Tram 1, 2, D, J. ❏ 45 Sch.
Fascinating collection of precious artefacts and relics. See **Hofburg**.

ÖSTERREICHISCHE NATIONALBIBLIOTHEK Josephsplatz 1.
❏ 1000-1600 Mon.-Sat., 1000-1300 Sun. (May-Oct.).
U Stephansplatz. Bus 2A. Tram 1, 2, D, J. ❏ 30 Sch.
*2.5 million books including the priceless collection of Prince Eugene of
Savoy. See* **A-Z**.

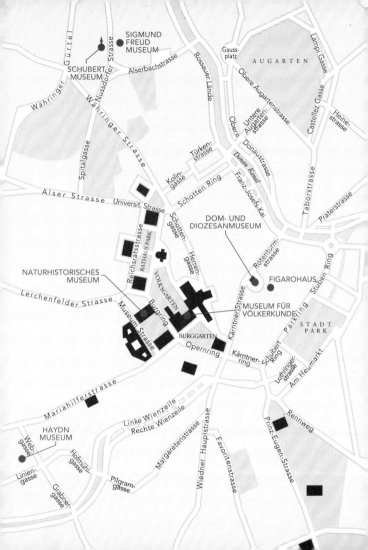

SIGMUND
FREUD
MUSEUM

SCHUBERT
MUSEUM

AUGARTEN

Gauss-platz

Lampi Gasse

Rossauer Lände

Castellez Gasse

Heine-strasse

Alserbachstrasse

Währinger Gürtel

Währinger Strasse

Nussdorfer Strasse

Spitalgasse

Obere Augartenstrasse

Untere
Augarten-
strasse

Obere Augarten-strasse

Donaustrasse

Taborstrasse

Praterstrasse

Türken-strasse

Donau Kanal

Kolin-gasse

Franz-Josefs-Kai

Schotten Ring

Alser Strasse   Universit. Strasse

Schotten-gasse

DOM- UND
DIOZESANMUSEUM

NATURHISTORISCHES
MUSEUM

Lerchenfelder Strasse

Reichsratsstrasse

RATHAUS PARK

VOLKSGARTEN

Burgring

Museum Strasse

Herren-gasse

Rotenturm-strasse

FIGAROHAUS

MUSEUM FÜR
VÖLKERKUNDE

Kärntner Strasse

Stuben Ring

STADT
PARK

Parkring

BURGGARTEN

Opernring

Kärntner-
ring

Schubert Ring

Lothringer-strasse

Am Heumarkt

Mariahilferstrasse

HAYDN
MUSEUM

Linke Wienzeile

Rechte Wienzeile

Magaretenstrasse

Wiedner Hauptstrasse

Favoritenstrasse

Rennweg

Prinz-Eugen-Strasse

Webg-gasse

Hofmühl-gasse

Linien-gasse

Grabner-gasse

Pilgram-gasse

MUSEUM FÜR VÖLKERKUNDE Heldenplatz, Neue Burg.
❏ 1000-1300 Mon., Thu.-Sat., 1000-1700 Wed., 0900-1300 Sun.
U Mariahilferstrasse. Tram 1, 2, D, J. ❏ 30 Sch.
15,000 objects including Emperor Maximilian's Mexican collection and artefacts from Captain Cook's voyages in the South Seas.

NATURHISTORISCHES MUSEUM Maria Theresien Platz.
❏ 0900-1700 Wed.-Sun. U Mariahilferstrasse. Bus 2A, 3A.
Tram 1, 2, D, J.
Minerals, fossils, skeletons, plants and a giant topaz weighing 117 kg!

DOM- UND DIÖZESANMUSEUM Rotenturmstrasse 2.
❏ 1000-1600 Wed.-Sat., 1000-1300 Sun. U Stephansplatz. Bus 1A.
A collection of sacred art dating from the Middle Ages to the present day, including works by Kessel, Maulbertsch and Rottmayer.

FIGAROHAUS Schulerstrasse 8.
❏ 1400-1600 Tue.-Fri., 1400-1800 Sat., 0900-1300 Sun. & hol.
Entrance in Domgasse. U Stephansplatz. Bus 1A. ❏ Free.
Mozart lived here for three years with his wife and son and composed the Schauspieldirektor, *not, as commonly thought, Figaro. See* **WALK 1**.

SCHUBERT MUSEUM Nussdorferstrasse 54.
❏ 1000-1215, 1300-1630 Tue.-Sun. U Nussdorferstr. ❏ Free.
This house was the birthplace of Schubert (see **A-Z***) and has been preserved virtually unaltered. Manuscripts and memorabilia are on display.*

SIGMUND FREUD MUSEUM Berggasse 19.
❏ 0900-1300 Mon.-Fri., 0900-1500 Sat., Sun. U Schottentor. ❏ 30 Sch.
Freud (see **A-Z***) lived here from 1891-1938 and you can see the famous couch, photographs and other memorabilia.*

HAYDN MUSEUM Haydngasse 19.
❏ 1000-1200, 1300-1630 Tue.-Sun. Bus 57A. Tram 52, 58. ❏ Free.
This is the house in which Haydn (see **A-Z***) composed* The Creation *and* The Seasons *and where he lived until his death in 1809.*

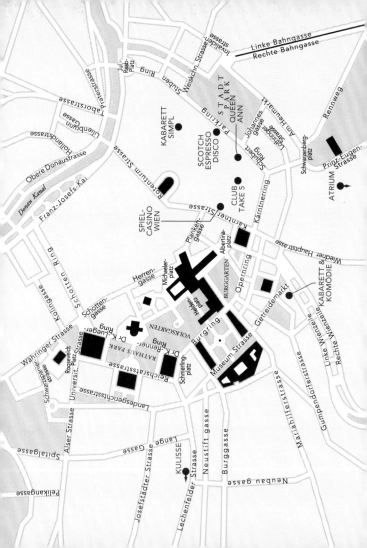

SPIEL-CASINO WIEN Kärntner Strasse 41.
❑ From 1700 daily. U Karlsplatz. ❑ 170 Sch (worth 200 Sch of chips).
State-owned casino with American and French roulette, chemin de fer and blackjack. Formal dress and passport required.

QUEEN ANN Johannesgasse 12.
❑ 2100-0400 Mon.-Thu., 2000-0500 Fri., Sat. U Karlsplatz. ❑ Free.
This is the jet-set disco of Vienna. There is an adjoining cocktail bar and all the latest music.

CLUB TAKE 5 Annagasse 3A.
❑ 2200-0330 (Fri., Sat. until 0430). U Karlsplatz. ❑ Free.
Up-market disco appealing to slightly older revellers.

SCOTCH ESPRESSO DISCO Parkring 10.
❑ 2000-0200 (Fri., Sat. until 0400). Tram 1, 2. ❑ Free.
Luxurious, sophisticated and romantic, with prices to match.

ATRIUM Schwindgasse/Ecke Schwarzenbergplatz.
❑ 2030-0400 Thu.-Sat. U Karlsplatz. Tram D. ❑ 10 Sch.
Mixed clientele enjoy this relaxed disco, which is Vienna's oldest, in a maze of cellar rooms.

KABARETT SIMPL Wollzeile 36.
❑ 2200-0330. Bus 1A. Tram 1, 2. ❑ 100 Sch.
A typical old-style Viennese cabaret – great fun!

KULISSE Rosensteingasse 39.
❑ 2200-0330. Tram 9. ❑ Meal cost.
Political cabaret which also offers a good meal for 45-95 Sch.

KABARETT & KOMÖDIE Linke Wienzeile 4.
❑ 2200-0330. U Karlsplatz then 5 min walk. ❑ 100 Sch.
Austrian and foreign groups and soloists appear with cabaret, pantomine, revues and songs.

DONAUPARK

Wagramer Strasse

Alte Donau

Neue Donau

Donau

A 22

Reichsbrücke

A 22

DONAUINSEL

Handelskai

Handelskai

PRATER

Hauptallee

Donau Kanal

Schüttelstrasse

Erdberger Lände

A 23

A 23

STADTPARK

VOLKSGARTEN

Rennweg

BURGGARTEN

Gürtel

Obere Donaustrasse

Gürtel

Linke Wienzeile

Gürtel

Gentzgasse

Währinger Strasse

Hernalser Hauptstrasse

Gablenzgasse

Burggasse

Gürtel

Felber Strasse

Wien Fluss

Grünbergstrasse

Eichenstrasse

Edelsinnstrasse

Flötzersteig

Hadikgasse

Maxingstrasse

SCHÖNBRUNN PARK

LAINZER TIERGARTEN

Lainzer Strasse

STADTPARK Parkring 1.
❑ 24 hr. U Stadtpark. Tram 1, 2, J. ❑ Free.
Beautiful park to stroll amongst the many statues. Open-air concerts near the Kursalon café. See **WALK 4**.

DONAUPARK Wagramer Strasse.
❑ 24 hr. U Alte Donau. Bus 90A, 91A, 92A, 20B.
The second-largest park in Vienna. Laid out in 1967, it includes attractions such as the Donauturm (see **A-Z**) *and playgrounds. See* **A-Z**.

PRATER Vienna District II.
❑ 24 hr. Amusement park open Mar.-Nov.
U Praterstern. Bus 80A. Tram 1, N, O. ❑ Free.
Natural park covering 3200 acres and offering all kinds of sports amenities from jogging to football. Site of Volksprater amusement park and Riesenrad (see **A-Z**). *See* **CHILDREN**, **Events**, **A-Z**.

BURGGARTEN Opernring-Burgring 1.
❑ 24 hr. U Mariahilferstrasse. Bus 57A. Tram 1 ,2 ,D, J. ❑ Free.
Pleasant Hapsburg garden with the only open-air statue of Franz Joseph.

LAINZER TIERGARTEN St. Veiter-Türl & Lainzer Tor.
❑ 0800-dusk Wed.-Mon. (April-Nov.); 0600-1900 winter (Hermespark only). U Hütteldorf. Bus 55B, 60B. ❑ Free.
Woodland sanctuary where you can see red deer and wild boar. The restored Hermesvilla (1886) was once a retreat of Empress Elizabeth.

SCHÖNBRUNN PARK Schönbrunner Schlossstrasse.
❑ 0600-dusk. U Schönbrunn. Bus 15A. Tram 10, 58. ❑ Free.
500 acres of parkland behind the castle with fountains, statues, the Gloriette (see **A-Z**) *and a romantic folly. See* **Schönbrunn Palace**.

VOLKSGARTEN Dr Karl-Renner-Ring 1.
❑ 24 hr. U Volkstheater. Bus 48A. Tram 1, 2, D. ❑ Free.
Situated on the site of the fortifications blown up by the French, with several attractive monuments and the Tilgner Fountain. See **WALK 2**.

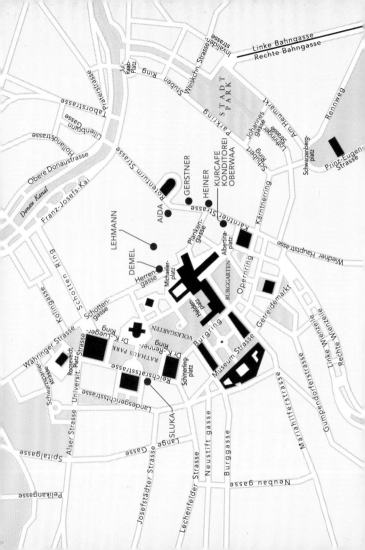

DEMEL Kohlmarkt 14.
❑ 1000-1800. U Stephansplatz.
The original Kaiserliche-Königliche Hofzuckerbackerei founded 200 years ago. The shop has a wonderful display of delicious cakes and confectionery. See **WALK 3**.

GERSTNER Kärntner Strasse 15.
❑ 0900-1900 Mon.-Sat. U Stephansplatz.
Once suppliers to the imperial court, now in modern premises but the pastries are still as good.

KURCAFE KONDITOREI OBERWAA Neuer Markt 16.
❑ 0900-1900 Mon.-Fri., 0900-1400 Sat. U Stephansplatz.
Housed in a renovated building, this café has beautiful packets of their own gift-wrapped chocolates – ideal for presents.

LEHMANN Graben 12.
❑ 0830-1930 Mon.-Sat. U Stephansplatz.
Pleasant to sit outside while sampling a pastry and coffee and watching the world go by.

SLUKA Rathausplatz 8.
❑ 0800-1900 Mon.-Fri., 0800-1730 Sat. Tram 1, 2, J.
Slightly off the beaten track but offering an enormous selection of coffees to sample along with their delicious cakes. In particular try their Obst Torten *(fruit tarts).*

AIDA Stock-im-Eisen Platz 2.
❑ 0700-2000 Mon.-Sat., 0900-2000 Sun. U Stephansplatz.
One of a chain that is found on most street corners just when you need to relax and take some refreshment.

HEINER Kärntner Strasse 21-23 & Wollzeile 9.
❑ 0730-1930 Mon.-Sat., 1000-1930 Sun. U Stephansplatz.
Delightful establishment which, thoughtfully, specializes in delicious pastries for diabetics.

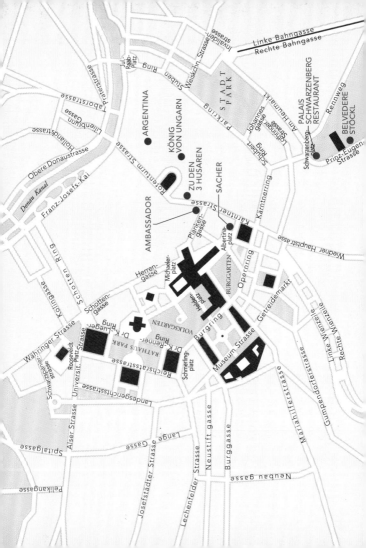

ARGENTINA Sonnenfelsgasse 17.
❑ 1900-2400 Mon.-Sat. ❑ Expensive.
Nouvelle cuisine *in one of the oldest parts of Vienna.*

AMBASSADOR Neue Markt 5.
❑ 1200-2400. U Stephansplatz. ❑ Expensive.
Luxury restaurant in one of the city's top hotels.

ZU DEN 3 HUSAREN Weihburggasse 4.
❑ 1800-0100 Mon.-Sat. Closed July-Aug. (4 weeks). U Stephansplatz.
❑ Expensive.
A monument to traditional Viennese cuisine in a grand setting of antiques, tapestries and flowers. Veal specialities.

KÖNIG VON UNGARN Schulerstrasse 10.
❑ 1130-1500, 1800-2400 Sun.-Fri. U Stephansplatz. ❑ Expensive.
Seasonal Viennese and international cuisine. Specialities are cold hors d'oeuvres and Viennese pastries.

SACHER Philarmonikerstrasse 4.
❑ 1200-1500, 1800-2330. U Karlsplatz. ❑ Expensive.
Long-established restaurant in this famous hotel where you may well rub shoulders with celebrities in the red dining room. Try the Tafelspitz *(see* **Food***), served with herb sauce, and the* Sacher Torte.

BELVEDERE STÖCKL Prinz-Eugen-Strasse 25.
❑ 1200-1500, 1800-2400 (summer 1200-2400). Tram D. ❑ Expensive.
Situated in the grounds of the Palais Schwarzenburg. In summer the attractive gardens form a delightful backdrop for diners.

PALAIS SCHWARZENBERG RESTAURANT
Schwarzenbergplatz 9.
❑ 1100-1430, 1800-2300. Tram D. ❑ Expensive.
The most beautiful restaurant in Vienna with a view of the palace park from the terrace. Sophisticated Viennese and French cuisine.

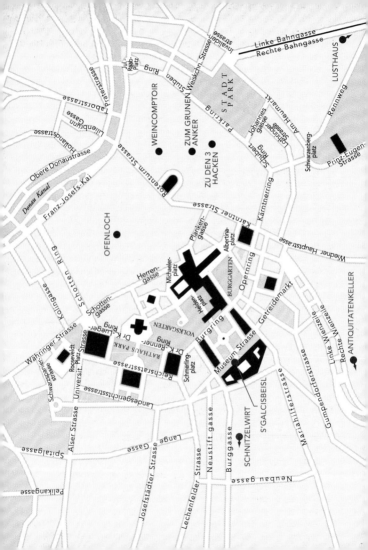

ZUM GRUNEN ANKER Grünangergasse 10.
❏ 1800-2400 Mon.-Fri. U Stephansplatz. ❏ Moderate.
*Viennese Beisl (see **Eating Out**) with Italian specialities.*

OFENLOCH Kurrentgasse 8.
❏ 1000-2400 Mon.-Sat. U Stephansplatz. ❏ Moderate.
*Viennese specialities (see **Food**), turn-of-the-century decor.*

ANTIQUITATENKELLER Magdalenenstrasse 32.
❏ 1800-0100. Closed Aug. U Kettenbrückengasse. ❏ Moderate.
Traditional Viennese food and classical music in a beer-hall atmosphere.

WEINCOMPTOIR Bäckerstrasse 6.
❏ 1000-2400 Mon.-Fri. U Stephansplatz. ❏ Moderate.
Excellent wines and good food in a beautifully renovated cellar.

S'GALCISBEISL Messepalast.
❏ 1100-2400 Mon.-Fri., 1800-2400 Sat. Closed Jan.-Mar.
U Mariahilferstrasse. ❏ Moderate.
Viennese and Bohemian food inside the old walls of the Imperial Stables.

LUSTHAUS Freudenau 54.
❏ 1100-2300 Thu.-Tue. (kitchen 1200-1430, 1800-2300). Bus 80A.
❏ Inexpensive.
*Once the Emperor's hunting lodge and now a very pleasant spot to linger
over a meal, especially in summer.*

SCHNITZELWIRT Neubaugasse 52.
❏ 1000-2200 Mon.-Sat. (hot food 1130-1400, 1730-2200).
U Lerchenfelderstrasse. ❏ Inexpensive.
*Largest schnitzels (see **Food**) in Vienna, so bring a substantial appetite!*

ZU DEN 3 HACKEN Singerstrasse 28.
❏ 0900-2400 Mon.-Fri., 1000-1500 Sat. Closed mid-June to mid-July.
U Stephansplatz. ❏ Inexpensive.
One of the last old taverns (Gasthauser) in Vienna's first district.

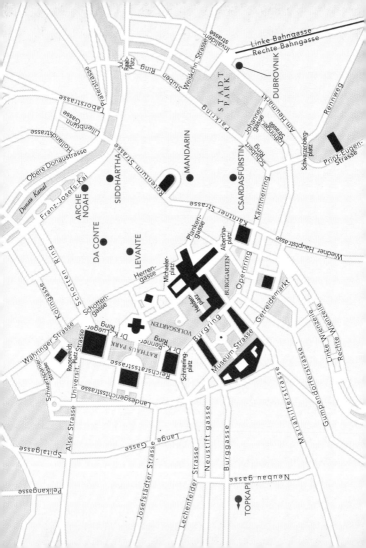

Linke Bahngasse
Rechte Bahngasse

DUBROVNIK

STADTPARK

Parkring

MANDARIN

CSARDASFURSTIN

Rennweg

Schwarzenberg-platz

Prinz-Eugen-Strasse

Kärntnerring

Wiedner Hauptstrasse

SIDDHARTHA

Rotenturm Strasse

Karntner Strasse

Planken-gasse

Albertina-platz

Opernring

Getreidemarkt

Jul. Raab-Platz

Weiskchn. Strasse

Invalidenstrasse

Am Heumarkt

Johannes-gasse

Lothringer Strasse

Schubert Ring

Sieben Ring

Praterstrasse

Taborstrasse

Lilienbrunn Gasse

Hollandstrasse

Obere Donaustrasse

Donau Kanal

Franz-Josefs-Kai

ARCHE NOAH

DA CONTE

LEVANTE

Herren-gasse

Michaeler-platz

Helden platz

BURGGARTEN

VOLKSGARTEN

Schotten-gasse

Burgring

Museum Strasse

Schotten Ring

Kolingasse

Schwarzspanierstrasse

Währinger Strasse

Roosevelt

Universit. Platz

RATHAUS PARK

Dr. Lueger-Dr. Karl Ring

Dr. Renner-Ring

Reichsratsstrasse

Schmerling-platz

Alser Strasse

Landesgerichtsstrasse

Lange Gasse

Josefstädter Strasse

Lechenfelder Strasse

Neustift gasse

Burggasse

Neubau gasse

Mariahilferstrasse

Gumpendorferstrasse

Linke Wienzeile

Rechte Wienzeile

Spitalgasse

Pelikangasse

TOPKAPI

DA CONTE Kurrentgasse 12.
❏ 1200-1500, 1800-2400 Mon.-Sat. ❏ Expensive.
Many consider this to be the best Italian restaurant in town. Delicious fresh fish and mussels and a delightful ambience.

TOPKAPI Burggasse 70.
❏ 1100-2400. U Volkstheater. ❏ Moderate.
Turkish specialities at reasonable prices and in pleasant surroundings.

DUBROVNIK Am Heumarkt 5.
❏ 1130-1430, 1800-2330. U Stadtpark. ❏ Moderate.
The most popular Yugoslav restaurant in town. Very good meat dishes and live music daily from 1930-2330.

CSARDASFÜRSTIN Schwarzenbergstrasse 2.
❏ 1900-0100 Mon.-Sat. ❏ Moderate.
One of the more up-market Hungarian restaurants in the city.

ARCHE NOAH Seitenstettengasse 2.
❏ 1200-1500, 1800-2400 Mon.-Sat. ❏ Moderate.
One of Vienna's few kosher restaurants, set in one of the liveliest areas.

SIDDHARTHA Fleischmarkt 16.
❏ 1130-1500 Mon.-Sat., 1130-1500 Sun. ❏ Moderate.
Up-market vegetarian restaurant with plush, red leather armchairs, candles and linen napkins. Large choice of dishes.

MANDARIN Singerstrasse 11.
❏ 1130-1430, 1730-2330. ❏ Inexpensive.
Long-established Chinese restaurant with consistently good Szechuan and Cantonese cuisine. The midday menu is good value for money.

LEVANTE Wallnerstrasse 2.
❏ 1130-2230. ❏ Inexpensive.
Excellent value for money. A mixture of Turkish, Greek and Middle-Eastern food. Tables outside in summer.

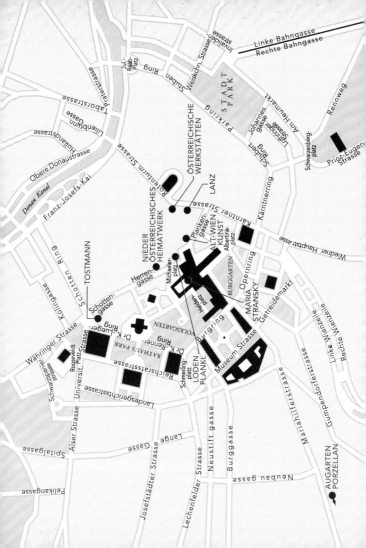

Linke Bahngasse
Rechte Bahngasse
Invalidenstrasse
Lessinggasse
Weidlich. Strasse
Stuben Ring
Jul. Raab-Platz
Parkstrasse
Obere Donaustrasse
Taborstrasse
Lilienbrunn Gasse
Hollandstrasse
Rotenturm Strasse
Franz-Josefs-Kai
Donau Kanal
STADT PARK
Parking
Am Heumarkt
Johannes Gasse
Lothringer Strasse
Schubert Ring
Schwarzenberg platz
Prinz-Eugen Strasse
Rennweg
ÖSTERREICHISCHE WERKSTÄTTEN
LANZ
NIEDER ÖSTERREICHISCHES HEIMATWERK
ÖSTERREICHISCHES HEIMATWERK
Planken gasse
Kärntner Strasse
ALT-WIEN KUNST
Albertina platz
Kärntnering
Wiedner Hauptstrasse
Annagasse
TOSTMANN
Schotten Ring
Kolingasse
Herren gasse
Michaeler platz
Helden platz
BURGGARTEN
Opernring
MARIA STRANSKY
Getreidemarkt
Schotten gasse
Dr. Lueger Ring
VOLKSGARTEN
Burgring
Dr. Renner Ring
Museum Strasse
Währinger Strasse
Schwarzspanier strasse
Roosevelt platz
Universit. Platz Strasse
RATHAUS PARK
Reichsratsstrasse
Schmetting platz
LODEN PLANKL
Landesgerichtsstrasse
Mariahilferstrasse
Linke Wienzeile
Rechte Wienzeile
Gumpendorferstrasse
Alser Strasse
Spitalgasse
Pelikangasse
Josefstädter Strasse
Lange Gasse
Lechenfelder Strasse
Neustift gasse
Burggasse
Neubaugasse
AUGARTEN PORZELLAN

See **Opening Hours**.

LANZ Kärntner Strasse 10.
U Stephansplatz.
Top-quality classical Austrian clothing, mainly for women.

LODEN PLANKL Michaelerplatz 6.
Bus 2A.
*Loden coats, jackets, suits, hats and knitwear (see **Best Buys**).*

TOSTMANN Schottengasse 3A.
U Schottentor.
*Dirndl (see **Best Buys**) and all that goes with it for day or night, winter or summer.*

ÖSTERREICHISCHE WERKSTÄTTEN Kärntner Strasse 6.
U Stephansplatz.
From Michaela Frey jewellery to horn combs via beeswax candles.

NIEDER ÖSTERREICHISCHES HEIMATWERK
Herrengasse 6.
Lower Austrian handicrafts and regional costumes.

AUGARTEN PORZELLAN Mariahilferstrasse 99 &
Stock-im-Eisen Platz 3-4. U Stephansplatz.
This famous porcelain, manufactured in the Schloss Augarten since the 18thC, is not cheap but these retail outlets are worth a look.

MARIA STRANSKY Hofburgpassage 2.
Bus 2A.
Traditional Viennese petit point in a variety of forms.

ALT-WIEN KUNST Bräunerstrasse 11.
U Stephansplatz.
This antique shop specializes in good glass, porcelain and Biedermeier furniture.

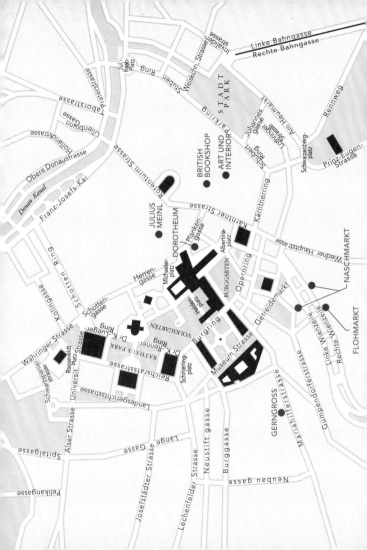

Linke Bahngasse
Rechte Bahngasse
Invalidenstrasse
Weiskirchn. Strasse
Jul. Raab-Platz
Stuben Ring
Parkring
S T A D T P A R K
Am Heumarkt
Johannesgasse
Lothringer gasse
Rennweg
Schubert Ring
Schwarzenbergplatz
Prinz-Eugen-Strasse
BRITISH BOOKSHOP
ART UND INTERIOR
Peterstrasse
Taborstrasse
Obere Donaustrasse
Hollandstrasse
Lilienbrunn Gasse
Donau Kanal
Franz-Josefs-Kai
Rotenturm Strasse
JULIUS MEINL
DOROTHEUM
Planken gasse
Kärntner Strasse
Kärntnerring
Albertinaplatz
Operngasse
Wiedner Hauptstrasse
Schottenring
Schottengasse
Herrengasse
Michaelerplatz
Heldenplatz
BURGGARTEN
VOLKSGARTEN
Getreidemarkt
NASCHMARKT
FLOHMARKT
Wahringer Strasse
Kolingasse
Dr Karl-Lueger Ring
Dr Renner Ring
Burgring
Museum Strasse
Linke Wienzeile
Rechte Wienzeile
Roosevelt Platz
Universit. Platz
RATHAUS PARK
Rathausplatz
Schmerling platz
Reichsratsstrasse
Schwarzspanierstrasse
Alser Strasse
Landesgerichtsstrasse
Josefstädter Strasse
Lange Gasse
Lechenfelder Strasse
Neustift gasse
Burggasse
Neubau gasse
GERNGROSS
Mariahilferstrasse
Gumpendorferstrasse
Spitalgasse
Pelikangasse

Miscellaneous

DOROTHEUM Dorotheergasse 17.
❑ 1000-1800 Mon.-Fri., 0830-1200 Sat. Auctions from 1400.
U Karlsplatz.
*Auction house for art and antiques originally founded in 1707 by
Joseph I. See* **WALK 3**.

FLOHMARKT (FLEA MARKET) End of Naschmarkt.
❑ 0800-1800 Sat. U Kettenbrückengasse.
*Something for everyone and every budget. And don't forget – bargaining
is all part of the fun!*

NASCHMARKT Link/Rechte Wienzeile.
❑ From 0800 daily. Access at Karlsplatz end.
*You are sure to succumb to the charm of everyday Austrian life at this
lively, colourful fruit-and-vegetable market.*

ART UND INTERIOR Seilerstätte 28.
U Stephansplatz.
*An interesting collection of paintings, furniture, glass and porcelain from
throughout the centuries.*

JULIUS MEINL Graben 19, and throughout the city.
U Stephansplatz.
*A good-quality supermarket chain with fresh produce and reasonable
prices – have a browse through their wine selection.*

GERNGROSS Mariahilferstrasse 38-48.
U Mariahilferstrasse. Tram 52, 58.
*A good-quality department store selling everything you might want, from
sausages to high fashion.*

BRITISH BOOKSHOP Weihburggasse 8.
U Stephansplatz.
*A bookshop with a very comprehensive selection of English and
American books, plus videos and cassettes.*

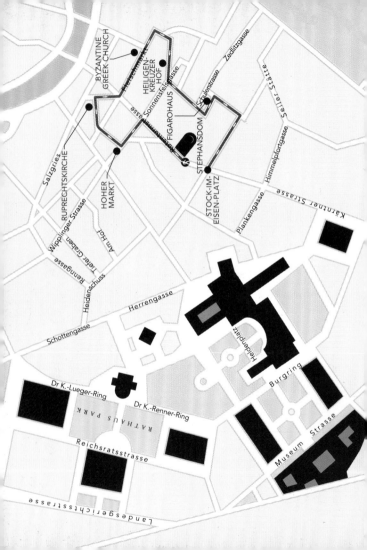

BYZANTINE
GREEK CHURCH

Zedlitzgasse

HEILIGEN-
KREUZER
HOF

Schulerstrasse

Seiler Stätte

Sonnenfelsgasse

FIGAROHAUS

STEPHANSDOM

Salzgries

RUPRECHTSKIRCHE

STOCK-IM-
EISEN-PLATZ

Himmelpfortgasse

HOHER
MARKT

Plankengasse

Wipplinger Strasse

Kärntner Strasse

Tiefer Graben

Rennegasse

Am Hof

Heidenschuss

Herrengasse

Schottengasse

Heldenplatz

Dr K.-Lueger-Ring

Burgring

Dr K.-Renner-Ring

RATHAUS PARK

Reichsratsstrasse

Museum Strasse

Landesgerichtsstrasse

The Inner City

1hr 30 min.

Start in Stephansplatz, the central point of the inner city. St. Stephen's Cathedral, Stephansdom (see **CHURCHES**, **A-Z**), is Vienna's principal landmark, its steeple rising to a height of 137 m. There is a lift up to the Pummerin (the huge bell made from melted-down Turkish cannons) in the north tower, from where there is a good view of the entire city.

From Stephansplatz, Rotenturmstrasse runs down to the Danube Canal. The second turning to the left after passing the Archbishop's Palace, on the corner of Stephansplatz and Wollzeile, leads to the Hoher Markt (see **A-Z**), once the centre of the Roman fortress of Vindobona. Roman remains can be seen here under the square (entrance at No. 3). At the east end of the square is the Ankeruhr, a clock which plays a tune accompanied by a parade of figures at noon. Judengasse leads to the right off the square to the Ruprechtskirche (see **CHURCHES**, **A-Z**), the earliest-recorded church in Vienna, said to have been founded in AD 740. Turn right from Ruprechtskirche into Seitensattengasse, past the synagogue, and then right into Rabensteig which leads you along the Fleischmarkt. This is one of the oldest streets in Vienna – recorded as early as 1220. In the 18thC Greek merchants settled here, and at No. 13 is the neo-Byzantine Greek church. Just before it Greichengasse branches off to the left. The Fleischmarkt runs into Postgasse where the main post office (see **A-Z**) is situated. Turn right and, a little way along, right again into Schonlaterngasse. Where this street turns to the right you have a good view over one of the oldest parts of the city. Through a turreted gate you can enter the Heiligenkreuzer Hof, one of the most peaceful spots of the city. The monastery was started in the 13thC and finally completed in the 18thC. Return through the gate you entered, into Schonlaterngasse once more, and continue into Sonnenfelsgasse. Directly opposite is a lane, Windhagg, that takes you through to Beckerstrasse. Apart from having a number of beautiful old houses to boast of, this street also has a number of good Viennese taverns and wine bars. Turn right, along Beckerstrasse, and on the left-hand side there is another small lane, Essigg, which leads into Wollzeile (a good shopping street). Cross over into Strobelgasse, carry straight on and then turn left into Domgasse, where the (incorrectly) named Figarohaus (see **MUSUEMS 2**) stands at No. 25 (it was *Der Schauspieldirektor* that Mozart (see **A-Z**) composed here and not the *Marriage of Figaro*). Turn right into Grunangergasse and walk along it until you nearly reach the end. On the right is the entrance to a series of charming courtyards leading to Blutgasse. This complex provides an interesting example of how the Viennese lived in the 17th and 18thC. At the end of Blutgasse turn right into Singerstrasse and continue along here to finish the walk

at Stock-im-Eisen-Platz at the junction of Kärntner Strasse (see **A-Z**) and Graben. The square takes its name from a nail-studded stump that has been standing here since around 1533. It is said that travelling black-smiths hammered a nail in for good luck before moving on to ply their trade elsewhere (see **Stock-im-Eisen**).

MARIA AM GESTADE

MORZINPLATZ

Salzgries

Fleischmarkt

Sonnenfelsgasse

Schulerstrasse

Zedlitzgasse

Seiler Stätte

Rotenturmstrasse

JUDENPLATZ

FÜTTGASSE

Wipplinger-Strasse

Himmelpfortgasse

AM HOF

Plankengasse

Kärntner Strasse

Tiefer Graben

Renngasse

SCHOTTENKIRCHE

Schottengasse

Herrengasse

Herdplatz

SCHOTTENGASSE

BURGTHEATER

Dr-K.-Lueger-Ring

TEMPLE OF THESEUS

VOLKSGARTEN

Burgring

Dr-K.-Renner-Ring

R A T H A U S P A R K

VOTIVKIRCHE

NEUES RATHAUS

Reichsratsstrasse

PARLIAMENT

Museum Strasse

Landesgerichtsstrasse

Parliament to Morzinplatz

1 hr 30 min.

Start from the Parliament (see **BUILDINGS 2**), seat of the Bundersammlung (Federal Assembly), constructed by Theophil Hansen. Opposite is the Volksgarten (see **PARKS & GARDENS**) with the Temple of Theseus. Carrying on into Dr Karl-Lueger-Ring you will see the Neues Rathaus (see **BUILDINGS 2**) on the left across the Rathaus Park. Facing it, on your right, is the Burgtheater (see **BUILDINGS 2**) founded in the time of Maria Theresa and rebuilt after being completely gutted by bombs during the war. Further on to the left is the University which was founded in 1365 and is the second-oldest in German-speaking territory. Opposite is the relic of the Old Fortifications, the Mölkerbastei, with a number of old Viennese houses. At No. 8 is the Beethoven Memorial Room (see **Beethoven, Beethoven Museums**). North of the University on Rooseveltplatz is the neo-Gothic facade of the Votivkirche built in 1853 after an assassination attempt on the young Franz Josef's life. Today it is in poor repair. Turn right into Schottengasse, in the direction of the Schottenkirche (see **CHURCHES, A-Z**) that dominates the newly renovated Freyung. On this square stands the Palais Ferstl which is connected to Herrengasse by a smart shopping arcade. Continue along Freyung into Heidenschuss until you reach Am Hof (see **A-Z**) where Roman remains have been found and can be seen in the Fire Brigade Museum at No 9. Walk anti-clockwise around the square to take the second turning on the right, Drahtgasse, into Judenplatz where Mozart (see **A-Z**) lived in 1783 and 1785. From here take Füttgasse, crossing Wipplingerstrasse into Stoss in Himmel to Passanerplatz. Here stands the 14thC Gothic edifice of Maria am Gestade (see **CHURCHES, A-Z**). Walking along Salvatoregasse will take you past the Renaissance portal of the 14thC chapel of the Old City Hall. Turn left into Marc Aurel-Strasse leading down to Morzinplatz adjacent to the Danube Canal. Here stood the infamous Hotel Metropole, HQ of the Gestapo in Vienna from 1938-45. It featured in several scenes of the Carol Reed film *The Third Man*.

From here, if you have enough energy left, you can climb the Ruprecht Stiege into the so-called Bermuda Triangle (see **Nightlife**) and pick up **WALK 1** along the Fleischmarkt, or visit one of the numerous restaurants for some well-earned refreshment.

Messepalast to Opera

2 hrs.
Start the walk at the Messepalast, which was formerly the imperial stables and is now the showplace of various trade exhibitions. It faces the Maria-Theresien-Platz, flanked on the right by the Kunsthistorisches Museum (see **ART GALLERIES**, **A-Z**), home to an outstanding collection of early Dutch painters, 17thC Flemish masters and painters of the Venetian School. Facing it on the left is the Naturhistorisches Museum (see **MUSEUMS 2**) with collections of the material from the graves and mines at Hallstatt, a collection of

meteorites and the famous *Venus of Willendorf*. In the centre of the square is the Maria Theresa monument showing a flattering likeness of the Empress at the age of 35. Walk straight ahead, over the Burgring, until you reach the Burgtor, which in 1934 became Austria's monument to the Unknown Soldier. From here there is a view across Heldenplatz towards the Hofburg (see **BUILDINGS 1**, **A-Z**), the winter residence of the Hapsburgs. Carry straight on across the square, passing on your right the Neue Burg, until you reach the passage leading to the square

known as In der Burg. This constitues the real heart of the Hofburg, with a bronze statue of the Emperor Francis. Head straight on through the Michaeler Tor, a grand passage and gateway, to Michaelerplatz. In the middle of this passage is the entrance to the Imperial apartments. From Michaelerplatz there is a good view down the Kohlmarkt, and on the left-hand corner of this street and the square is the Looshaus (see **BUILDINGS 2**), designed by Adolph Loos in 1910 in protest against the Art-Nouveau style of the time. Facing it on the right is the Michaelerhaus, home to the young Haydn (see **A-Z**) from 1750-57. To the right of this is the

Michaelerkirche (see **CHURCHES**, **A-Z**). Walk down the Kohlmarkt where medieval charcoal sellers once had their stalls. Chopin stayed at No. 9 from November 1830 until July of the following year. You will also find the famous Café Demel (see **PASTRY SHOPS**) on the left as you walk down. At the bottom turn right along Graben (see **A-Z**) whose main feature is the baroque Dreifaltigkeitssäule (Trinity Column), commonly known as the Pestsäule (see **A-Z**). It was erected in memory of up to 150,000 Viennese who died during a particularly virulent outbreak of bubonic plague in 1679. On the left-hand side of Graben is the Peterskirche (see **CHURCHES**, **A-Z**), rebuilt in its present form in 1702 on the site of one of the oldest churches in Vienna. Just before you reach Stephansplatz, turn right into Dorotheergasse. On the left as you go up is the Dorotheum (see **SHOPPING 2**), a state-run auction house and pawn shop founded in 1707. At the top, turn left into Augustinerstrasse towards Albertinaplatz, a busy square which contains a statue of Mozart (see **A-Z**). Facing this, on the ramp leading to the Augustiner Bastei, is a statue of Archduke Albrecht. Behind this is the Albertina (see **ART GALLERIES**, **A-Z**), housing a fine collection of graphic art. At the back of the Bastei is the Burggarten (see **PARKS & GARDENS**), once the promenade of the imperial family. Turning left onto the Burgring will take you past a statue of Goethe and then to the Staatsoper (see **BUILDINGS 2**, **A-Z**), the Opera House built between 1861-69 and the end point of this walk.

Michaelerkirche

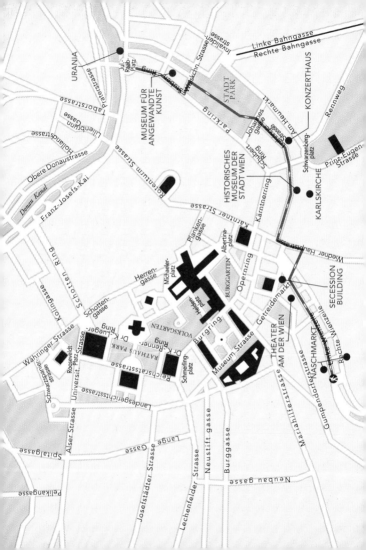

URANIA

Linke Bahngasse
Rechte Bahngasse

Lilienbrunn Gasse
Taborstrasse

Praterstrasse

Obere Donaustrasse

Hollandstrasse

Donau Kanal

Franz-Josefs-Kai

Rotenturm Strasse

Jul.-Raab-Platz

Invalidenstrasse

Weisskirchn. Strasse

STADT PARK

Parkring

Am Heumarkt

KONZERTHAUS

Rennweg

MUSEUM FÜR ANGEWANDTE KUNST

Johannes Gasse

Schubert Ring

Schwarzenberg platz

Prinz-Eugen-Strasse

HISTORISCHES MUSEUM DER STADT WIEN

KARLSKIRCHE

Kärntner Strasse

Kärntnering

Wiedner Hauptstrasse

Planken-gasse

Albertina-platz

Herren-gasse

Michaeler-platz

BURGGARTEN

Opernring

SECESSION BUILDING

Schotten Ring

Schotten-gasse

Heldenplatz

VOLKSGARTEN

Burgring

Getreidemarkt

Wåhringer Strasse

Kolingasse

Roosevelt platz

Dr Lueger Ring

RATHAUS PARK

Dr Renner Ring

Schmerling platz

Museum Strasse

THEATER AN DER WIEN

NASCHMARKT

Linke Wienzeile

Rechte Wienzeile

Gumpendorfer Strasse

Mariahilferstrasse

Universit. Platz

Reichsratsstrasse

Schwarzspanier strasse

Alser Strasse

Landesgerichtsstrasse

Spitalgasse

Pelikangasse

Lange Gasse

Josefstädter Strasse

Lechenfelder Strasse

Neustift gasse

Burggasse

Neubau gasse

Naschmarkt to Urania

2 hrs.

Start at Kettenbrückengasse underground station. The Naschmarkt is built over the river Wien and is flanked by the Linke and Rechte Wienseile. Stay on the Linke Wienseile in the direction of the city. The buildings to look out for along the way are Nos. 38 and 40 – both designed by Otto Wagner – and the Theater am der Wien, an important part of Vienna's theatrical history. It was built on the site of the theatre where *The Magic Flute* was first performed. At the crossing of the Linke Wienseile and the Getreidemarkt is the Secession Building (see **Secession**) with its gilded iron dome of laurel leaves, nicknamed the 'Golden Cabbage'. It is the home of, among other things, Klimt's Beethoven frieze (see **Beethoven, Klimt**). Facing away from the Secession building, crossing the Linke and Rechte Wienseile into Treitlstrasse over the Wiedner Hauptstrasse, you come to Karlsplatz, dominated by the Karlskirche (see **CHURCHES, A-Z**), the baroque master-piece of J. B. Fischer von Erlach. At the northeast corner of Karlsplatz is the Historisches Museum der Stadt Wien (see **MUSEUMS 1, A-Z**) which houses a collection of painting and objects relevant to the history and culture of the city. From here turn right down Lothringerstrasse into the Schwarzenbergplatz. At the intersection stands the statue of Prince Karl Phillip zu Schwarzenberg, allied commander at the battle of Leipzig. Carry on down Lothringerstrasse, past the Konzerthaus and the Akademietheater on the right, over Johannesgasse and into the Stadtpark (see **PARKS & GARDENS**). Laid out in 1862, it contains several statues including those of Bruckner, Schubert (see **A-Z**) and Strauss the Younger (see **A-Z**). Through the park turn left onto Weisskirchnerstrasse and then right onto the Stubenring. Continuing ahead, on the right-hand side you pass the Museum für Angewandte Kunst (see **A-Z**), founded in 1864. Adjacent to this is the Academy of Applied Art where Kolo Moser and Kokoschka both studied and later taught. Further on is the former War Office and in front is a statue of Marshall Radetzky. Opposite is a small square behind which is the Post Office Savings Bank by Otto Wagner. The Ring ends on Julius Raab Platz and to the right is the Urania, an observatory with conference and lecture halls. From here, take a restful boat tour of the Danube Canal or simply wander back to the city centre.

Accidents & Breakdowns: In the case of a minor accident follow the normal procedure of exchanging names, addresses and insurance details. If there are complications or someone has been injured call the police (tel: 133). Both Austrian motoring organizations have 24-hour services: ÖAMTC, tel: 120; ARBÖ, tel: 123. See **Driving**, **Emergency Numbers**.

Accommodation: The official categories are as follows:
Hotels – the grading system is strictly controlled by the state and ranges from five-star (luxurious) to one-star (modest).
Pensions – smaller, simpler, bed and breakfast establishments which are often family run and good value.
Seasonal Hotels – student hostels which are converted into hotel-type accommodation during holiday months with services usually provided by the students.
Finding accommodation can often be difficult from Easter to October so it is always advisable to reserve a room. Reservations are binding for hoteliers and travel agents as well as the visitor who stands to lose a deposit in case of cancellation. For a list of hotels contact the Tourist Office (see **Tourist Information**). If you are stuck for a room on arrival contact one of the following:
Zimmernachweis at Westbahnhof, tel: 835185 (0615–2300).
Zimmernachweis at Sudbahnhof, tel: 652168 (0615–2200).
Airport Tourist Office, tel: 7770-2617 (0830-2300 summer, 0830-2200 winter).
There are also accommodation services on the south and west motorways and at the DDSG docking station on the Danube (see **A-Z**).
See **Camping & Caravanning**, **Youth Hostels**.

Airport: Vienna's international airport, Wien-Schwechat, is located 19 km southeast of the city centre. The modern airport building has a bank, bars, restaurants, shops, a post office and tourist office. There is a bus every 20 min from the City Air Terminal at the Hilton Hotel (0600-1900, or later to accommodate evening flights) which takes 30 min and costs 50 Sch. A shuttle bus service operates every 30 min between Westbahnhof and the airport via Sudbahnhof 0700-1900 (50 Sch).

There is an hourly train service (0730-2030) between the airport and City Air Terminal and Wien Nord. Taxis charge between 250 and 300 Sch for a journey between the city and the airport.

Akademie der Bildenden Künste: The Academy of Fine Arts was founded in 1692 by Peter von Strudel but did not move into its present premises until 1876. It houses an exceptional collection of old masters. Works of particular interest include Hooch's *Conversation Piece*, a portrait by Rembrandt, and a triptych by Bosch entitled *The Last Judgement*. The Academy, which is world-famous, trains designers, architects and graphic artists. Hitler tried to enrol here in 1907 but he failed the entrance exams. See **ART GALLERIES**.

Albertina: The Albertina Collection of Graphic Arts was founded by Duke Albert of Saxony-Tescha (Maria Theresa's son-in-law) in 1768. The collection is the most important of its kind in the world and includes over 50,000 drawings and 1,200,000 original prints. Because of the delicate nature of a lot of the works, some of the drawings on display are copies of the originals. On display are drawings such as Dürer's *The Hare* and *The Praying Hands* and Raphael's *Madonna with the Pomegranate*. Rubens' portraits of his family can also be seen. The Austrian Film Museum is housed in the same building and shows films of historic or artistic value, all in their original languages with German subtitles. See **ART GALLERIES, WALK 3**.

Am Hof: The largest square in the city centre features several buildings of interest, including the Burghers' Armoury at No. 10 which now houses the Fire Brigade; the Zur Goldenen Kugel at No. 11; and the Urbanihaus at No. 12. The square is dominated by the baroque facade of the Kirche Am Hof (see **A-Z**), also called the Church of the Nine Choirs of Angels. In the centre stands the Mariensäule (Golden Ball), originally erected in 1667 to commemorate the delivery of the city from the Swedes during the Thirty Years' War. The Babenbergs' castle stood on the site at No. 7, which explains the name of the square ('Am Hof' means 'at the court') before the Hapsburgs moved to the Hofburg (see **BUILDINGS 1, A-Z**). See **WALK 2**.

Ankeruhr: See **Hoher Markt**.

Augustinerkirche:
Augustinerstrasse 3. U Stephansplatz.
Built for the Augustinian Canons in the
14thC and of extremely simple design.
It was the scene of the wedding of
Emperor Franz Josef and Elizabeth of
Bavaria in 1845. It houses the beautiful
tomb of Maria Christina (Maria
Theresa's daughter), the work of the

Am Hof

Italian Antonio Canova (1805), and a splendid gold-and-white organ case. It also contains the Heart Vault where the hearts of all the Hapsburgs (starting from 1619) are kept in silver urns.

Baby-sitters: Ask at your hotel reception or contact either of the following: Babysitter-Zentrale, Herbststrasse 6-10, tel: 951135 (0800-1430 Mon.–Fri.); Österreichischer Akademischer Gastedienst (Student Society Service), Mohlgasse 20, tel: 5873525. The cost is about 50 Sch per hr (minimum 3 hr) plus transport (taxi after 2300).

Banks: See **Money**.

Beethoven, Ludwig van (1770-1827): Born in Bonn, Beethoven visited Vienna briefly in 1787 and took lessons from Mozart (see **A-Z**), but it was late 1792 before he returned to study with Haydn. By 1800 he was the leading young musician on the Viennese scene with a growing reputation abroad. During the first years of the new century he began to realize that he was going deaf but continued to compose and conduct with increasing difficulty until his death. He seldom lived long in one apartment and it has been estimated that he had over 40 changes of address during his 35 years in Vienna (see **Beethoven Museums**). His remains lie in the Zentralfriedhof (see **A-Z**) next to those of Schubert (see **A-Z**) and Brahms (see **A-Z**).

Beethoven Museums: The famous composer (see **Beethoven**) was well known for changing residences frequently and the following are now museums open to the public:
Pasqualati House, Mölkerbastei 8 (see **WALK 2**).
House of the Heiligenstadt Testament, Probusgasse 6.
Eroica Haus, Döblinger Hauptstrasse 92.
Beethoven Apartment, Laimgrubengasse 22.
The museums open 1000-1215, 1300-1630 Tue.-Sun., apart from the Beethoven Apartment, which is open only by prior arrangement.

Belvedere-Schlösser: The two baroque palaces, connected by formal gardens, were built for Prince Eugene by Lucas von Hildebrandt between 1700 and 1723. Known as the Upper (*Oberes*) and Lower (*Unteres*) Belvederes, the former houses the Österreichische Galerie des 19. und 20. Jahrhunderts and the latter the Österreichisches Barockmuseum (see **ART GALLERIES**). The Orangery adjoining the Barockmuseum also contains the Museum Mittelalterlicher Österreichischer Kunst (Museum of Medieval Austrian Art). The most magnificent feature of the palace is the Gold Salon in the Lower Belvedere. The Austrian State Treaty, ending the Allied occupation and establishing Austria as a free and neutral state, was signed in the palace in 1955. See **BUILDINGS 1**.

Best Buys: Amongst the most popular souvenirs to bring back from Vienna are items of the Austrian national dress: dirndl (fitted-bodiced dresses with low necks and full skirts); lederhosen (leather breeches); and the Alpine hats with or without feathers that no respectable Austrian is without. If you find it a little too much for adults, buy the children's versions – they can be really cute. Loden garments, although not particularly cheap, are excellent quality. Antiques are plentiful and

also constitute a good buy in Vienna which offers a varied choice of authentic pieces. Augarten porcelain and petit-point embroidery feature in all the souvenir shops although quality can vary and you generally get what you pay for. The Austrians are excellent woodworkers and make original, brightly painted toys. Porcelain clocks, glassware and wrought-iron work are also popular souvenirs. A sure way of reliving memories of your holiday once you are back at home is by sipping an after-dinner apricot or plum brandy (*barack* and *slivovitz* respectively) while listening to a cassette of one of the many classical composers – both liqueurs and tapes are on sale all over Vienna. Chocolate or the sweet, thick, nougat liqueur called Mozart's Liqueur, is ideal for those with a sweet tooth. Or take back some of the coffee for which Vienna is so famous (see **Drinks**). See SHOPPING 1 & 2, **Shopping**.

Bicycle Hire: Cycling is popular in Vienna and there are numerous bicycle lanes marked out throughout the city. The ARGUS map, available in all bookshops, will enable you to plan a bike tour. The Tourist Office official hotel guide indicates which hotels and pensions have special facilities for riders. Organized sightseeing tours lasting up to 2 hr 30 min depart from Salztorbrücke bike rentals by Schwedenplatz on the right shore of the Danube Canal (cost 150 Sch). You can hire bikes from the following places (cost about 30 Sch per hr): Prater 133 (near the roller coaster); Vivariumstrasse 8; and Waldgasse 47.

Brahms, Johannes (1833-97): Born in Hamburg, Brahms settled in Vienna in the autumn of 1863, where he became a freelance teacher. In the following years he completed a number of piano and chamber works, including *A German Requiem*, before producing his First Symphony in 1876. The Second Symphony appeared shortly after, and during the 1880s, in addition to his Third and Fourth symphonies, he composed a stream of piano works, chamber music and songs. He toured often and widely and was greatly admired wherever he went. His music combined the austerity of classical forms with the lyricism of the Romantic spirit. He is buried in the Zentralfriedhof (see **A-Z**).

Budget:

Breakfast in a hotel	from 65 Sch.
Dish of the day	from 45 Sch.
Coffee	25-35 Sch.
Theatre ticket	150-700 Sch.
Pint of beer	from 25 Sch.
House wine	from 25 Sch for 25cc glass.
Wine	50–70 Sch for a good bottle of table wine.

Burggarten: See PARKS & GARDENS.

Burgkapelle: See **Hofburg.**

Burgtheater: See BUILDINGS 2, WALK 2.

Buses: Buses in Vienna are modern and spacious. If you plan to use them frequently you should invest in the 10 Sch transport map, available from the transport information centres, to get a clear idea of routes (these are also marked on the free Tourist Office map but the print is extremely small). The fare structure is the same as for the trams (see **A-Z**). Late-night buses have recently been introduced on Fridays and Saturdays and on the eves of public holidays (1230–0400, 25 Sch – passes are not valid on these services). All the night buses originate from Schwedenplatz. See **Transport**.

Cameras & Photography:
Films are expensive in Vienna as
is developing, although the latter
is of good quality, even in the
one-hour developing shops.
Photography is allowed in most
museums but usually without the
use of either a flash or a tripod
which makes it fairly difficult. You
are not allowed to take pictures in
the Schönbrunn Palace (see
BUILDINGS 1, **A-Z**) or the Spanish
Riding School (see **A-Z**).

Camping & Caravanning: There are four well-equipped camp
sites within the Vienna region:
Campingplatz der Stadt Wien – (Wien West I), Hüttelbergstrasse 40, tel:
941449 (open mid-June to mid-Sep.); (Wien West II), tel: 942314 (open
all year round).
Campingplatz der Stadt Wien – (Wien Sud), Breitenfurter Strasse 269,
tel: 869218. (open end of May to mid-Sep.).
Schwimmbad Camping Rodaun, An der Au 2 (Rodaun), tel: 884154.
(open mid-Mar. to mid-Nov.).
Campingplatz Schloss Laxenburg, Munchendorfer Strasse, tel: 0223-
671333 (open mid-Mar. to end Oct.).
Expect to pay about 50 Sch per adult, 30 Sch per child and 46 Sch for a
car or place for a tent. For further details contact the Tourist Office (see
Tourist Information) and ask for their Camping/Youth Hostel brochure
or the camp site itself. Alternatively, write to Österreichischer Camping
Club, Schubertring 8, 1010 Vienna.

Car Hire: There is no difference in price between local and international car-hire agencies so it is generally advisable to go to an international company who are used to dealing with foreign clients. There are
numerous branches all over the city and most of them are represented
at the airport (see **A-Z**). Ask at your hotel reception or look in the

yellow pages for the nearest office. The minimum age for hiring a car is usually 21 and you must have held a valid driving licence for at least a year. Paying by credit card exempts you from leaving a deposit. See **Accidents & Breakdowns**, **Driving**.

Chemists: The chemists (Apotheken) in Austria have a monopoly over the dispensing of all medicines. The equivalent to Boots the Chemist in Britain is Drogerie Markt (DM) where you will find everything from rat poison to shampoo but no aspirins or prescription service. Most chemists keep normal shop opening times (0900-1800 Mon.-Fri., 0900-1200 Sat.) but they also operate a rota system so you will always find at least one open. The addresses of the nearest are listed outside each chemist should you need their services at night or on Sunday. Alternatively, phone 1550. See **Health**.

Children: Vienna is a clean, safe place for children and there is plenty for them to see and do. Although it is not usually convenient to take them out at night, there are several baby-sitting organizations. Baby food, nappies and other products are available in chemists (see **A-Z**), Drogerie Markt and supermarkets at more or less the same prices as in the UK. Pram access to most museums and public places is usually available. See **CHILDREN**, **Baby-sitters**.

Climate: Vienna has clearly defined seasons with reasonably hot (although sometimes rainy) summers (24°C) and cold, crisp winters (1°C) with snow. Spring is often sunny but chilly, while autumn may be sunny and warm. In winter take prcautions when driving (see **Driving**).

Climbing: For information about climbing contact the ÖAV (Österreichische Alpinverein), Wallfischgasse 12, tel: 512693 or 5124373.

Complaints: If you have a complaint you should first try to sort it out with the manager or owner of the establishment involved before taking it up, in writing, with the Tourist Office. If it is about the price of a room, for example, include a photocopy of the receipt, without which your complaint will not be treated. Do not hesitate to contact the police (see **A-Z**) for serious problems. See **Tourist Information**.

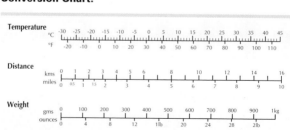

Consulates:

UK – Jauresgasse 12, tel: 756117/18
R. of Ireland – Landstr Hauptstrasse 2, Hilton Centre, tel: 7524246
Canada – Dr Karl-Lueger–Ring 10, tel: 5333691
USA – Gartenbaupromenade 2, tel: 51451

Conversion Chart:

Temperature

°C -30 -25 -20 -15 -10 -5 0 5 10 15 20 25 30 35 40 45
°F -20 -10 0 10 20 30 40 50 60 70 80 90 100 110

Distance

kms 0 1 2 3 4 5 6 8 10 12 14 16
miles 0 0.5 1 1.5 2 3 4 5 6 7 8 9 10

Weight

gms 0 100 200 300 400 500 600 700 800 900 1kg
ounces 0 4 8 12 1lb 20 24 28 2lb

Crime & Theft: Vienna is a safe city as far as crime goes but it is still sensible to take precautions. Leave any valuables in the hotel safe (not in your room) and do not invite theft (by leaving a wallet sticking out of a back pocket, items on display in a parked car, etc.). If you are the victim of a theft you should go first to the police who will issue you with a statement which you will need for your consulate or embassy (in the case of loss of a passport) or for your insurance company at home. See **Consulates**, **Emergency Numbers**, **Insurance**, **Police**.

Currency: The Austrian monetary unit is the schilling (Sch) which is divided into 100 groschen (g). Coins are 2, 5, 10 and 50 groschens; 1, 5, 10 and 20 schillings. Notes in circulation are 20, 50, 100, 500, 1000 and 5000 schillings. 1 and 10 schilling coins are the most useful small change for telephones and stamp machines. See **Money**.

Customs: The Austrian lifestyle is fairly relaxed and slow, well-ordered and conservative. Greetings are considered to be very important, as are courtesies, so the following words will be useful: *Guten Tag* (good day); *Guten Abend* (good evening); *Gute Nacht* (good night); *bitte* (please); *danke schön* (thank you). Do not be disconcerted if you find yourself the object of careful scrutiny as it is intended to be neither aggressive nor rude. You will find that most people speak good English and are only too pleased to help a visitor in need.

Customs Allowances:

Duty-free Into:	Cigarettes	or	Cigars	or	Tobacco	Spirits	Wine
AUSTRIA	200		50		250 g	1*l*	2.1*l*
UK	400		100		500 g	1*l*	2.25*l*

Danube: The Danube flows below the central part of Vienna, not through it as do rivers in most capitals. Only on very clear days can one possibly describe its rather muddy waters as being 'blue'. It is very well regulated and as recently as 1981 a second channel was cut through the inundation flats. The earth from this was used to create a 20-km-long, 200-m-wide island, which is now a recreation area. There is also a lot of commercial river traffic, and large barges flying the flags of the Eastern European countries are a common sight.

Dentists: See **Health**.

Deutschordenskirche: Singerstrasse 7. U Stephansplatz. Founded by the Order of the Teutonic Knights, a German order dating back to 1190, and dedicated to St. Elizabeth. The church escaped dramatic baroque alterations and has remained in its Gothic form. It has a splendid Flemish altarpiece and carved organ loft. The walls are decorated

by the Knights' shields. A lift in the adjacent courtyard takes you up to the Schatzkammer des Deutschen Ordens, the small but interesting treasury of the wealthy knights.

Disabled People: Vienna is a relatively easy city to visit for those with reduced mobility or confined to a wheelchair. At the entrance of most museums and public places there is a blue sign with a white wheelchair indicating wheelchair access. For a brochure about suitable hotels published by the Club Round Table 14 Wien, write to Dr Dieter Grosseger, 2100 Korneuburg, Wienerstrasse 125, tel: 0226-25671 or ask at the Tourist Office (see **Tourist Information**). See **Health**, **Insurance**.

Doctors: See **Health**.

Dom- und Diözesanmuseum: See MUSEUMS 2.

Dominikanerkirche: Postgasse 4. U Stephansplatz/Schwedenplatz. This impressive early-baroque building dates from 1632 and is the third church on this site which was first consecrated by the Dominicans in the 13thC. The interior has very interesting 17th and 18thC frescoes and you should also notice the chapels and high altar.

Donaupark: With an area of 247 acres this is the second-largest park in Vienna. It was created in 1964 out of a converted city rubbish dump, as the site for the Vienna International Garden Show. A railway runs around the gardens; there is an artificial lake with a theatre, which can hold 4000, on its banks and a chair lift runs between the Old and New Danube, offering won-derful views over the park. The park also contains the Donauturm (see **A-Z**), and there are playgrounds, a small animal enclosure and a bird-house. See PARKS & GARDENS.

Donauturm: Situated in Donaupark (see PARKS & GARDENS, **A-Z**), this is Vienna's tallest building. It has a viewing terrace and two revolving restaurants and is open 0900-2400 (summer), 1000-2300 (winter); cost 40 Sch, child 30 Sch.

Dorotheum: See SHOPPING 2, WALK 3.

Drinks: East Austria, and in particular the Vienna and Wachau districts and Burgenland, constitute the country's main wine-producing regions. The majority are young, light white wines that are best tasted in the *Heuriger* (wine tavern) of the vineyard itself as soon as the wine comes out (autumn). Among the more well-known white wines are Gumpoldskirchen, Klosterneuburg (from the Augustinian monastery –

see **EXCURSION 2**, **A-Z**), Kremser and Dürnsteiner. They are often drunk mixed with sparkling mineral water to produce a refreshing (but potent) drink called *G'spritzter*. Red wines are less common but Blaufrankisch, from the Burgenland, is considered to be the best. Beer is very popular and most of the brands you will come across will be Austrian. Try *Gösser* (a popular brew from Styria) and *Ottakringer* (a Viennese beer). For those who want to sample something a little stronger *slivovitz* (plum brandy) or *barack* (apricot brandy from Hungary) will probably fit the bill. And then, of course, there is the lengthy list of coffees to choose from, all of which are served with a glass of water. Coffee was originally introduced to the Viennese by the Turks and a Turkish coffee will be served (thick, sweet and strong) from its copper pot. If you simply ask for a coffee you will probably be served with a *Brauner* (strong with milk) but the choice is never-ending, from *Kaisermelanger* (black with an egg yolk) through to *Eiskaffee* (cold with vanilla ice cream) and includes the more familiar cappuccino, espresso and mocha.

Driving: If you plan to take your own car into Austria, you will need a national or international driving licence, green-card insurance, the log book, a nationality car sticker, a warning triangle and a first-aid kit. Drivers must be at least 18 years old. Driving is on the right-hand side and you must give priority to traffic on the right unless otherwise stated although trams always have priority in Vienna (even when coming from the left). Seat belts are obligatory and children under 12 are not allowed in the front seat. The speed limits are as follows: 50 km/hr in built up areas; 100 km/hr (60 for caravans) on ordinary roads; 130 km/hr (70 for caravans) on motorways. The Austrians have severe penalties for drinking-and-driving offenders (maximum blood alcohol level 0.8%). Care should be taken when driving during the winter months because of fog and snow. If you are planning to drive in the country in winter you should carry snow chains for your tyres. Driving within the inner city is not really recommended as parking is not easy and although there are several large underground car parks, e.g. Am Hof Square, Karlsplatz, Neuer Markt, Opera, these are often full. You can park for up to 90 min in a limited-parking zone (marked out by blue lines on the road and constituting most of the 1st district) if you display a voucher. These are available from tobacconists (*Tabak-Trafik*), banks, garages and Tourist Offices and they come in three colours – red for 30 min, blue for 60 min and green for 90 min. Illegally parked cars are often towed away by the police.

There are two main car associations in Austria. Österreichischer Automobil-, Motorrad- und Touring-club (ÖAMTC), Schubertring 1-3,

A-1010, tel: 72990. For traffic and road information, tel: 1590 (recorded message in English and German). The ÖAMTC are affiliated to the AA. Auto-, Motor- und Radfahrerbund Österreichs (ARBÖ), Mariahilfer Strasse 180, tel: 8535357.

Both leaded and unleaded (*Blei–frei*) petrol is widely available, and several petrol stations open late on the outskirts of town. Petrol is quite expensive at 10 Sch/litre for super and 7.50 Sch for diesel.

See **Accidents & Breakdowns**, **Car Hire**, **Transport**.

Drugs: All forms of narcotic drugs are strictly illegal in Austria.

Eating Out: Vienna offers a wide range of eating places, from luxurious restaurants to Würstel stands (hot-dog stands). The different categories include restaurants (serving either typically Austrian or international fare); *Beisel* (the equivalent of an inn/bistro serving simple Austrian dishes); *Heurigen* (wine taverns that usually also serve food); cafés (a real Viennese café serves hot dishes or snacks all day); and snack bars (try the Nordsee chain for original fish salads and open sandwiches). Restaurants are generally open 1200-1500 for lunch and from 1800 for dinner. Establishments serving food all day indicate this on a board reading 'Ganztags warme Kueche'. The best place to go if you want to wander round and choose a place you like the look of is the area known as the Bermuda Triangle (see **Nightlife**) although you will need to reserve in the more popular ones. The bill will include a 10-15% service charge although it is customary to leave a tip if you are satisfied with the service and food. Note that while most restaurants accept major credit cards and Eurocheques, you should check before you eat in a *Beisel* or *Heuriger*. The Tourist Office (see **Tourist Information**) publish a pamphlet listing under star gradings all establishments serving food ranging from five-star luxury to one-star modesty. And if you still cannot find something to eat you can always pop into a butcher's shop for rolls which can be filled with a variety of cooked meats. See **CAFÉS**, **HEURIGEN**, **RESTAURANTS**, **Food**, **Heurigen**.

Eisenstadt: 37 km from Vienna. Pop: 10,000. Eisenstadt has been the provincial capital of the Burgenland since 1924 and is best known

as the town where Josef Haydn (see **A-Z**) lived for 30 years as Kapellmeister in the service of the Esterházy family. His house in Haydngasse has been converted into a museum containing mementoes of his life and works, and the composer's mausoleum can be visited in the Bergkirche above the town. The castle, Schloss Esterházy, was originally built between 1388-92 but was redesigned in baroque style in the 17thC. The facade looking over the garden dates from the early 19thC. The main interest for visitors is the Haydn Room where the musican performed many of his compositions. Besides the Bergkirch mentioned above, it is also worth visiting the Franziskanerkirche (1630) which contains the Esterházy family crypt. See **EXCURSION 1**.

Electricity: 220V. Plugs are either oval with two pins or round with two pins and earthed for more powerful appliances. Visitors from the UK will need an adaptor and those from the US and Canada will need an adaptor/converter.

Emergency Numbers:

Police	133
Fire Brigade	122
Ambulance	144
Emergency Doctor (1900-0700)	141

Ephesos Museum: See **MUSEUMS 1**.

Events: The following is a list of the most important events and festivals that take place every year in Vienna. For specific details contact the Tourist Office (see **Tourist Information**), although they are not allowed to make reservations – to do this you should apply to the establishment itself or book through a travel agency.
January: The Philharmonic Orchestra's New Year concerts.
February: Carnival with numerous balls (including those of the Philharmonic Orchestra and the Masked Ball at the Imperial Court).
March: Haydn Festival; The Spring Marathon; Viennale Film Festival.
April-October: Waltz and operetta concerts throughout Vienna.
May-June: Vienna International Music Festival.

May: Spring Festival at the Prater (see **PARKS & GARDENS, A–Z**).
June: Procession of floral floats in the Prater
July-August: Summer Festival of Music; International Youth Music Festival.
September: Viennese International Trade Fair.
November: Schubert Festival; Antique Fair.
December: The Imperial Ball at the Hofburg.

Figarohaus: See **MUSEUMS 2, WALK 1**.

Food: Austrian cuisine consists of a potpourri of mid-European dishes with influences primarily from Hungary, Czechoslovakia and Yugoslavia. The dishes are often quite heavy and an Austrian would traditionally eat a main meal at lunchtime with snacks in the afternoon and something lighter in the evening. A meal will often start with soup: *Leberknödel* (broth with chicken-liver dumplings), or *Gulyassuppe* or *Wiener gulasch* (from Hungary, the latter being less heavily spiced with paprika than the former) are among the most popular.

Typical Viennese main course specialities include: *Wiener Schnitzel* (veal, or sometimes pork, escalope in breadcrumbs, served with potatoes or cucumber salad); *Backhendel* (deep-fried chicken pieces); *Tafelspitz* (a boiled-beef dish); *Gulyas* (beef stew with paprika, originally from Hungary); and fresh-water fish, such as *Forellen* (trout) or *Karpfen* (carp) usually stuffed or fried in breadcrumbs. A common

accompaniement to these dishes is *Geröstete* (sautéed potatoes) and a sauce such as *Schnittlauchsauce* with chives or *Kren* (horseradish).

Desserts are varied and as rich as the main courses. Pancakes (*Palatschinken*) served with cream, chocolate, jam or hazelnuts (or a mixture); the famous *Apfelstrudel* – a must; dumplings stuffed with apricots or cream cheese; or one of the vast range of pastries (with or without extra cream!). See **RESTAURANTS, Eating Out**.

Franziskanerplatz: Singerstrasse/Weihburgg. U Stephansplatz. Bus 1A. This is one of the prettiest squares in the city. The country coaches used to set out from the hostelry Zum grünen Löwen at No. 6. The Franziskanerkirche, which has a Renaissance facade and a Gothic interior, was built between 1603 and 1611 by the Franciscan friars on the site of a 14thC Franciscan convent. The baroque organ dating from 1643 is the oldest in the city.

Freud, Sigmund (1856–1939): Freud was the founder of psychoanalysis and revolutionized our understanding of the subconscious and its effect on human behaviour. His theories were slow to gain recognition and enter common medical and cultural discourse, but he has since become a household name. He lived in the Berggasse 19 (see **MUSEUMS 2**) until the annexation of Austria by Hitler's Germany in 1938, when he fled to London.

Gloriette: This classical arcade, designed by Hetzendorf von Hohenberg in 1775, enjoys a commanding position overlooking the Schönbrunn park (see **PARKS & GARDENS**). It was commissioned by Maria Theresa (see **Hapsburgs**) as a war memorial.

Graben: A wide thoroughfare in the heart of the city which was once surrounded by baroque buildings and was the site of the flower and vegetable market. It is now a bustling pedestrian precinct lined with cafés. In the centre is the Pestsäule (see **A–Z**) and two fountains dating from the early 19thC. See **WALK 3**.

Grinzing: This former village surrounded by vineyards is now largely a northwest suburb of Vienna. Access is by tram 38. Although the vineyards are disappearing under new housing developments the area remains famous as the centre of the *Heurigen* (see **HEURIGEN**, **A–Z**) – either the new wine or the taverns which sell it – which attract thousands of thirsty tourists each year.

Gloriette

Guides: See Tourist Information.

Hapsburgs: The Hapsburgs were the ruling dynasty in the Austro-Hungarian Empire from 1276-1918. The most famous family members were: Rudolf IV the founder; Maria Theresa, mother of Marie Antoinette; and Franz Joseph who ruled from Vienna for 68 years. The dynasty came to an end in 1918 with the exile of Emperor Karl at the end of World War I.

Haydn, Joseph (1732-1809): Haydn was born at Rohrau in Lower Austria. He came from a modest, rural family and went on to become, towards the end of his life, one of the most famous musicians in Europe, and principal architect of the classical style. Contrary to the norm, Haydn managed to make a good living from his music. He eventually became Kapellmeister to the Esterházys in Eisenstadt (see **EXCURSION 1**, **A-Z**) and wrote a series of symphonies, operas, church and chamber music for his patrons. He was a friend of Mozart (see **A-Z**), and in 1792 took Beethoven (see **A-Z**) as a pupil. In 1791 and 1794-95 he visited London and produced his London Symphonies (Nos. 93-104). In 1795 he was re-employed by the Esteh$\acute{a}$zy family and composed a series of annual Masses and two choral works, *The Creation* (1798) and *The Seasons* (1801).

Haydn Museum: See MUSEUMS 2.

Health: Although Austria is not part of the EC, reciprocal health arrangements do exist which cover all or part of any medical treatment you might need. It is, however, highly recommended to take out a private health insurance before leaving home and your travel agent will be able to provide this. Your hotel should be able to give you the name of an English-speaking doctor or dentist or, failing that, enquire at your consulate (see **A-Z**). In the yellow pages doctors come under 'Ärzte'. If you need a dentist during the night or at weekends, tel: 5122078 for a tape recording of where to summon help. Vienna does not pose any particular problems healthwise – the food is good (if a little heavy), the tap water drinkable and the climate mild. The only point worth mentioning is the existence of ticks in some regions of Austria and notably in the Vienna Woods. These ticks are particularly hazardous as they are carriers of encephalitis. If you plan to do any hiking in spring you should be inoculated beforehand. If you do see a tick on your skin (it starts off as a red dot the size of a pinhead and gradually gets fatter) rub the area with oil before trying to pull it out. Do not leave the head in the skin. Seek medical advice if you have not been inoculated. See **Disabled People**, **Emergency Numbers**, **Insurance**.

Heeresgeschichtliches Museum: See MUSEUMS 1.

Heiligenkreuz: 34 km southwest of Vienna. Access is by bus from Wien-Mitte bus station. Famous for the Abbey of the Holy Cross founded in 1133, although most of the buildings date from the 17thC when it was reconstructed after having been destroyed by the Turks. Frederick II, the last Babenberg duke, is remembered on a gravestone in the chapterhouse. There are various illustrations and models on display in the Monastery Museum. Do not miss the splendid display of 300 red marble pillars in the cloisters. Tours 0900, 1000, 1100, 1330, 1430, 1530. 1100-1130, 1330-1730 Sun. & hol.

Heiligenstadt: U Heiligenstadt. Formerly a village, now best known as one of Beethoven's summer retreats (see **Beethoven**). At Probusgasse No. 6 is the house where the composer wrote his moving *Heiligenstadt Testament*, lamenting his increasing deafness. See **Beethoven Museums**.

Heurigen: The *Heurige* is a very old tradition. Vinters would hang a wreath of fir twigs over the doors of their inns or wine cellars to announce the arrival of their new wines (*Heuriger*) which could then be sampled. Today they serve wine all year although the best time to go is in the autumn. The main wine-growing villages around Vienna are Grinzing (see **A-Z**), Sievering, Neustift am Walde and Nussdorf, all of which are accessible by public transport. See **HEURIGEN**.

Hiking: The beautiful Wienerwald (Vienna Woods) stretch along the foot of the hills behind the city and are full of hiking routes (see **Health**). Freytag & Berndt hiking maps are useful. The area is easily accessible by trams D, 40, 41, 43, 49, 60 or U Hütteldorf.

Historisches Museum der Stadt Wien: Exhibits in the Historical Museum of Vienna trace the origins and development of Vienna from Neolithic settlements in the Danube basin to modern times. They include original stones from St. Stephen's Cathedral, collections of weapons, old house and traders's signs, Biedermeier paintings and furniture, Franz Grillparzer's apartments and Adolph Loos' living room set up with careful attention to detail. A favourite is the model of Vienna depicting life during the Hapsburg period. There is also a section of Art Nouveau by Austrian artists. See **MUSEUMS 1**, **WALK 4**.

Hofburg: The Imperial Palace of Vienna, the oldest parts of which date back to the 13thC, occupies an extensive area in the heart of the city. It was a winter palace for the Hapsburgs and has evolved into a network of buildings, courtyards, gardens and stairways in an array of different styles – Gothic, Renaissance, baroque, Rococo and Classical. Until 1918 it was the seat of the ruler of Austria and it is now the official seat of the Austrian President. The oldest section is clustered around the Swiss Court and includes the Burgkapelle, which was built by Frederick III in 1447 in Gothic style. It is the home of the Vienna Boys' Choir (see **A-Z**) who can be heard at High Mass on Sundays. The Schatzkammer, or Imperial Treasury, is near the chapel and houses the priceless Hapsburg crown which dates from AD 962 and is lavishly decorated with emeralds, sapphires and diamonds. Other exhibits include the Burgandian Treasure with artefacts from the Order of the Golden Fleece and a holy 9thC lance (see **MUSEUMS 1**).
The Imperial Apartments (Kaiserappartements) are magnificently decorated with tapestries and one can see the splendid silver tableware used by Franz Joseph and Elizabeth.
The Neue Burg is the latest addition to the Hofburg and houses four museums – Waffensammlung (see **MUSEUMS 1**), Ephesos Museum (see **MUSEUMS 1**), Museum für Völkerkunde (see **MUSEUMS 2**) and the Musikinstrumentensammlung. The Österreichische Nationalbibliothek

is housed in a wing stretching towards the Staatsoper (see **BUILDINGS 2, A-Z**) and is in baroque style by J. B. and J. E. Fischer von Erlach. The Winterreitschule (Winter Riding School) was also designed by J .E. Fischer von Erlach and is where the Spanish Riding School (see **CHILDREN, A-Z**) holds its displays in July and August. Another feature of the palace is the Stallburg, the stables for the Lippizaners, originally built as a residence for the King of Bohemia. Upstairs in the Stallburg is the Neue Galerie devoted to 19th and 20thC art by non-Austrians, including works by Degas, Van Gogh and Renoir. See **BUILDINGS 1, WALK 3**.

Hoher Markt: U Stephansplatz/ Schwedenplatz. Bus 1A, 2A, 3A. Tram 1, 2. This is the oldest square in Vienna, dating back to the city's earliest beginnings. It was here that Roman Emperor Marcus Aurelius died. The buildings around the square were largely rebuilt after heavy fighting in 1945. The fountain in the centre was originally erected by J. B. Fischer von Erlach. Another feature is the Ankeruhr, a splendid 1911 clock by the painter Franz von Matsch, which strikes noon accompanied by a procession of historical figures. See **WALK 1**.

Insurance: It is always advisable to take out travel insurance for a holiday abroad. Ask your travel agent for details. See **Crime & Theft, Driving, Health**.

Josephinum: Währinger Strasse 25/Van-Swieten-Gasse 3. 1100-1500 Mon.-Fri. U Schottentor. A medical museum housing a fascinating collection of wax anatomical models made in Florence 1775-85 at the request of Joseph II for the training of army doctors and surgeons.

Josephsplatz: Augustinerstrasse. U Stephansplatz. Bus 2A. This is perhaps the city's most attractive square. It is surrounded by late-baroque buildings, including the Österreichische Nationalbibliothek (see MUSEUMS 1, A-Z), the Spanish Riding School (see CHILDREN, A-Z), Palais Pálffy (see BUILDINGS 1) and Palais Pallavicini. The memorial in the centre is of Maria Theresa's son, Joseph II, dating from 1795-1806.

Kapuzinerkirche: Founded by Empress Anna in 1618, the church is almost totally devoid of ornamentation, in keeping with the vows of poverty that the Capuchin Order took. The entrance to the Kaisergruft (Imperial Burial Vault) lies on the left-hand side of the church. The nine vaults are arranged in chronological order, and a tour will lead you past the tombs of 138 members of the Hapsburg family covering the period 1633-1918. See CHURCHES.

Karlskirche: Another important baroque building designed by J. B. Fischer von Erlach and completed by his son. It was consecrated in honour of the 'Plague Saint' Charles Borromeo. The church is striking not only because of its size and situation, but also for its historical significance (it was commissioned by Karl VI to mark the end of the plague in 1713). All the countries which owed allegiance to the crown had to make a contribution to the costs – the city of Hamburg's contribution came from a fine imposed for the destruction of a chapel. It was built to an oval plan with a 72-m-high dome decorated by Rottmayr. In the middle of the facade is a pillared porch flanked by two columns depicting scenes from the life of the saint. See CHURCHES, WALK 4.

Karlsplatz: Dominated by the imposing Karlskirche (see CHURCHES,

A-Z), the square was completely renovated between 1969 and 1978. Otto Wagner's fine Art-Nouveau-style pavilions in green and gold form the Karlsplatz underground station and they have recently been restored to their former splendour. A bronze statue of Mark Antony drawn along by four lions, is outside. To the south is the ugly, modern Technisches Uni (somewhat marring the effect of the Karlskirche).

Kärntner Strasse: One of Vienna's central thoroughfares (partly pedestrianized) which joins Stephansplatz (see **A-Z**) with Karlsplatz (see **A-Z**), and is lined with shops, offices, hotels and cafés. At No. 37 is the Malteserkirche, a small Gothic 14thC temple with a neoclassical facade, dedicated to the Knights of St. John.

Kirche am Hof: The Church of the Nine Choirs on Am Hof (see **A-Z**) boasts a magnificently intricate early-baroque facade which was designed by the Italian Carlo Carlone in 1662. It was formerly a Jesuit church and it was from this balcony that the end of the Holy Roman Empire and the German Nation was announced on 6 August 1806. Inside there is a fine ceiling fresco by Maulpertsch.

Klimt, Gustav (1862-1918): Klimt was the foremost Secessionist painter (see **Secession**). His work is a variation on Art Nouveau and is easily recognized for its glittering Byzantine mosaic flavour. Among his most famous works are *The Kiss* and *Field of Poppies*. His paintings can be seen in various locations including the Österreichische Galerie des 19. und 20. Jahrhunderts in the Upper Belvedere (see **ART GALLERIES**, **Belvedere-Schlösser**).

Klosterneuburg: 13 km north of Vienna. Pop: 23,000. Access is by train from Franz-Josephs-Bahnhof or bus from Wien-Mitte station. This market town and centre of the major wine-producing area in Austria is famous for its Augustinian Abbey, founded in 1108. The Abbey and Romanesque church (1114-36) underwent continual modification right up to the 19thC. The Babenberg family were the first occupiers when they moved here from Melk (see **EXCURSION 2**, **A-Z**) although Charles VI had it rebuilt along the lines of El Escorial monastery near Madrid. The monastery's finest work is the altarpiece in the chapel of St. Leopold (Nicolas of Verdun, 1181). There is also an interesting museum (Stiftsmuseum) housing works such as the Babenburg family tree (Hans Part, 1489) and the white marble Madonna (c.1310). The museum is open 0930-1100, 1330-1700 Mon.-Fri. (winter until 1600); 1330-1600 Sat., Sun. & hol. 30 Sch, child 10 Sch. See **EXCURSION 2**.

Krems: 72 km northwest of Vienna. Pop: 23,000. A charming rustic town of courtyards and winding streets featuring some ancient houses and parts of the original fortifications. The most picturesque part of the town is what was formerly the village of Stein. Some fine examples of oriel windows can be seen – for example at Steinlanderstrasse 76 and the Rathaus (1548) at Obere Landstrasse 4. The parish church is one of the oldest baroque churches in the area and is richly decorated with 18thC frescoes, mostly by Martin Johann Schmidt. The Historisches Stadtmuseum is in a former Dominican monastery and has a collection of M. J. Schmidt's paintings as well as arms and ironwork from prehistoric to Roman times. The Weinbaumuseum is an interesting collection of artefacts of the region's wine industry. See **EXCURSION 2**.

Kunsthistorisches Museum: The Museum of Art was founded when it was realized that the Imperial collection, housed in Prince Eugene's former summer residence, had outgrown the premises. Today it constitutes one of the greatest collections of art from the Renaissance to the 19thC. As well as the world-famous Picture Gallery the museum's collections comprise the Egyptian and Oriental Collection, Antiquities, Sculpture and Applied Art, and Coins and Medals. The museum is overwhelming in its size and it is recommended that you plan your tour carefully (English guidebooks are for sale at the entrance) or visit the museum at least twice. Rubens, whose work was greatly influenced by the Venetian style, is particularly well represented (Rooms XIII and XIV). You can see the *Ildefonso Altarpiece* (1630-32) – one of the best-known works depicting the appearance of the Virgin – in Room XIII. A fine self portrait (1639, one year before his death) and his portrait of *Helen Fourment* (his second wife) also feature here. More than half of Bruegel the Elder's works can be seen in this gallery

(Bruegel Room – Room X) with his splendid *Fight between Carnaval and Lent* (1559) and vivid *The Return of the Hunters* (1565) among the most noteworthy. Other artists represented from the Dutch, Flemish and German Schools include Dürer (*Adoration of the Trinity*, 1511), Vermeer (*The Artist in his Studio*) and Rembrandt with his remarkable *The Artist's Mother as the Prophetess Hanna*. Out of an equally rewarding selection of works from the Italian, Spanish and French Schools it is perhaps worth noting Giorgione's *Three Philosophers* and a beautiful *Madonna* by Raphael. Room V features the striking colours of Carvaggio's *David with the Head of Goliath*. See **ART GALLERIES**.

Lainzer Tiergarten: See PARKS & GARDENS.

Lippizaner: See Spanish Riding School.

Lost Property: The general Lost Property Office is at Wasagasse 22, tel: 3166110 (0800-1300 Mon.-Fri.). Anything left on a train or at a station is sent to the central office at Westbahnhof. Finally, for objects left on public transport, contact Wiener Stadtwerke-Verkehrsbetriebe, tel: 659300. After three days, however, all objects from here are transferred to the office in Wasagasse (see above). If you lose a credit card, tel: 6589650.

Maria am Gestade: Dating back to 1158, St. Mary on the Banks was originally situated on the banks of the Danube, on an arm of the river that has long since disappeared, leaving the church inland. It was built on Roman foundations and suffered a long history of destruction and reconstruction before being rebuilt in the 14thC in its present state. The bell tower is a masterpiece of Gothic art and inside, the magnificent stained-glass windows date back to the 14thC. Note the fine quality of the two parts of the tryptich by Stiegen (1460) – *The Annunciation* and the *Coronation of the Virgin*. See **CHURCHES**, **WALK 2**.

Markets: See SHOPPING 2.

Mayerling: This is the hamlet where, on the night of 29/30 January

1889, Rudolph, the 29-year-old crown prince and his 17-year-old mistress, Baroness Mary Vetsera, supposedly committed suicide in the prince's hunting lodge. It was never known if it was a real suicide or an assassination. Franz Joseph had the hunting lodge destroyed and a Carmelite nunnery erected on its site.

Melk: 108 km from Vienna. Pop: 6000. A small town dominated by its magnificent Abbey, whose church interior is thought to be one of the finest examples of baroque style in Europe. The site was originally the seat of the ruling Babenberg family before they moved to Klosterneuburg (see **EXCURSION 2, A-Z**) and was given to the Benedictine monks in 1098. The monks turned it into a fortified abbey and it developed into a centre of learning, with a library containing over 80,000 volumes. The present-day construction, however, dates from the early 18thC and is attributed to Jakob Prandtauer. The remarkable interior of the church, damaged by a fire in 1974, features gold-and-marble decor and paintings by Troger and Rottmayr. See **EXCURSION 2**.

Michaelerkirche: This used to be the parish church of the Imperial Court and was also used for the funerals of important figures in Austrian history. Built in the first half of the 13thC in a late-Romanesque style, it was later enlarged in Gothic, baroque and neoclassic styles to give the present strange architectural hybrid. The facade by Koch is simple and austere and immediately attracts attention. The tomb of the 18thC poet, Pietro Metastasio, can be seen near the altar. See **CHURCHES, WALK 3**.

Money: Banks are open 0800-1500 Mon., Tue., Wed., Fri., 0800-1730 Thu. (smaller branches close 1230-1330). Money can be changed in most branches or in one of the numerous bureaux de change. Some of the more convenient ones are to be found at the following places: the airport (0630-2300); Westbahnhof (0700-2200); Sudbahnhof (0630-2200); City Air Terminal at the Hilton Hotel (0800-1230, 1400-1800); Reisebüro City on Stephansplatz (open Sun.); Karlsplatz (open weekends). Money can also be changed at hotels and Tourist Offices but exchange rates are not as good. You will need your passport when changing traveller's cheques which are accepted in some shops but try to avoid this, as rates of exchange are low. Eurocheques are a national form of payment and are widely accepted with a Eurocheque card although your passport may also be required as further proof of identity. See **Crime & Theft**, **Currency**.

Mozart, Wolfgang Amadeus (1756-91): Mozart began his tragically short life in Salzburg but as he grew up he became disgruntled with life and conditions there. At the age of 25, in 1781, he came to Vienna where his musical and financial fortunes were constantly in a state of fluctuation. This was illustrated in a remark made by Emperor Joseph II after the Viennese premiere of *Don Giovanni*: 'Lovely, divine, but no food for the teeth of my Viennese'. Mozart replied, 'They will have to learn to chew'. His Viennese years were nevertheless a period of personal happiness. Despite the great works he composed and performed here, he died in poverty and was buried in an unmarked grave outside the city walls (see **St. Marxer Friedhof**).

Museum Für Angewandte Kunst: Stubenring 5. 1000-1600 Tue., Wed., Fri.; 1000-1800 Thu.; 1000-1300 Sun. U Wien-Mitte. Bus 1A. Tram 1, 2. Founded in 1864, the Museum for Applied Art is one of the most important institutions of its kind in Europe. The exhibits cover the Medieval period to the 19thC and include furniture and *objets d'art*, glass, tapestries, clocks, Meissenware, Oriental carpets, Chinese bronzes and ceramic figures, Viennese porcelain and exhibits of *Jugendstil* design. See **WALK 4**.

Museum Moderner Kunst: The museum of Modern Art is housed in the beautiful baroque building of the Gartenpalais Liechtenstein (see **BUILDINGS 1**). The collection includes works of 20thC artists such as

Klimt (see **A-Z**), Picasso, Schiele, Magritte, Hamilton and Warhol. The surrealist section is particularly strong. See **ART GALLERIES**.

Music: See **Beethoven, Brahms, Events, Haydn, Mozart, Nightlife, Opera, Schubert, Strauss, Vienna Boys' Choir**.

Musikvereinsgebäude: Dumbastrasse 3. U Karlsplatz. Tram 1, 2, D, J. Commissioned by the Musikfreunde (Society of Music Lovers) in 1867 and designed by Thophil Hansen, this is the home of the Vienna Philharmonic Orchestra. The VPO's New Year's Day concert is broadcast world-wide every year from the famous Goldener Saal (Golden Hall) with its coffered ceiling and superb acoustics. See **BUILDINGS 2**.

Naturhistorisches Museum: See **MUSEUMS 2**.

Neue Burg: See **Hofburg**.

Neue Markt: In the centre of this busy square is the Donner-Brunnen, a fountain erected in 1734 and named after its designer, Georg Raphael Donner. The fountain has a statue of Providence surrounded by four naked figures representing four tributary rivers of the Danube (see **A-Z**): the Traun, Enns, Ybbs and March. At No. 4 is the Rauchmiller Palais with a facade by J. E. Fischer von Erlach. On the west side is the Kapuzinerkirche (see **CHURCHES**, **A-Z**) and Kaisergruft where 138 members of the Hapsburg family are buried.

Newspapers: Most international newspapers and magazines are available the day after publication, except for the *International Guardian, Financial Times, Herald Tribune* and some French national papers which are immediately available. See **What's On**.

Nightlife: Vienna is surprisingly lively at night and there is a pleasant, jovial, relaxed atmosphere. The most animated area is what is known as the Bermuda Triangle in the Old Town, the area between Morzin Platz, Stephansplatz and Kohlmarkt. This is where most of the fashionable cocktail and music bars are to be found interspersed with restaurants. For an evening in a *Heuriger* make your way out to Grinzing (see **A-Z**) on the tram fondly known as the 'Heurigen Express' (No. 38). A visit to the opera, concert hall or theatre is a must here and, although ticket prices are fairly high, there is no shortage of opportunities to see a performance. During the various 'seasons' make sure you reserve well in advance (see **Events**). See **BARS, HEURIGEN, NIGHTLIFE, RESTAURANTS 1 & 2**.

Opening Hours: In general:
Banks – 0800-1500 Mon., Tue., Wed., Fri., 0800-1730 Thu. (smaller branches close from 1230-1330).
Post Offices – 0800-1800 Mon.-Fri.
Shops – 0900-1800 Mon.-Fri., 0900-1300 Sat. (0900-1700 first Sat. in the month).

Opera: Opera in Vienna is taken extremely seriously and even people who have never entered the portals of the famous Staatsoper (see **BUILDINGS 2, WALK 3, A-Z**) are *au fait* with the machinations of the people who run it. This is probably due to the fact that it is state run and therefore paid for by the person in the street. The Opera House is on a par with La Scala of Milan and New York's Metropolitan, and produces some sensational performances. The Staatsoper is also the venue for the annual Opera Ball, once one of the most elegant of the Viennese balls, but which in recent years has become a protest ground for anti-establishment forces and the scene of some unpleasant riots.

Orientation: Vienna is divided into 23 districts. The first district covers the inner-city area and is surrounded, in concentric circles, by the other 22. In addresses these are represented as A-1010, A-1020, etc. On some street signs and maps you may see ß appearing in the middle of a word; this is always pronounced as 'ss'. You may also see 'ü' as 'ue', 'ä' as 'ae' and 'ö' as 'oe'.

Österreichische Galerie des 19. und 20. Jahrhunderts:
This collection of paintings of 19th and 20thC Austrian artists traces the development of *Jugendstil* and is housed in the Upper Belvedere (see **Belvedere-Schlösser**). The best sections of the gallery are on the top floors where you can see original paintings by Klimt (see **A-Z**). Schiele's (see **A-Z**) work is also on these floors. See **ART GALLERIES**.

Österreichische Nationalbibliothek: As well as the collection of 2.5 million books, the Austrian National Library contains special collections of globes, maps, papyri, manuscripts, a portrait and picture archive and music and theatrical collections. The library itself dates back to the 14thC although the building itself with its magnificent baroque hall was designed by J. B. and J. E. Fischer von Erlach in 1722-26, and is now linked to the Hofburg (see **BUILDINGS 1**, **A-Z**). The Music Collection (over 45,000 manuscripts and 98,000 scores) and Papyrus Collection are kept in the Albertina (see **ART GALLERIES**, **A-Z**) and the Theatrical Collection is in the Neue Burg. See **MUSEUMS 1**.

Palais Pálffy: See **BUILDINGS 1**.

Parking: See **Driving**.

Passports & Customs: A valid passport but no visa is needed for UK, USA and Canadian citizens. No vaccinations are required (see **Health**). Note that the duty-free allowances in **Customs Allowances** apply only to visitors from European countries.

Pestsäule: The popular name for the Dreifaltigkeitssäule (Trinity Column) in Graben (see **A-Z**), a baroque marble pillar erected in memory of those who died (between 30,000 to 150,000 according to various estimates) in the 1697 plague. See **WALK 3**.

Peterskirche: Although documentary evidence for a church on this

site only dates from 1137, Charlemagne is supposed to have founded one here in 792. The medieval church was restored several times before finally being replaced in the 18thC by the present building. Johann Lukas von Hildebrandt modelled the church on St. Peter's in Rome. The interior is considered to be the best example of baroque style in Vienna. Note the trompe l'oeil above the high altar and the magnificent fresco by Rottmayr on the dome. See **CHURCHES**, **WALK 3**.

Petrol: See **Driving**.

Police: The police in Vienna wear dark green uniforms with black trousers and all are armed. Traffic police wear white caps and drive white cars. The motorbike police that patrol the motorways wear black leather jackets. If you are stopped you will be expected to pay a fine immediately – they make no concessions for tourists even though they are helpful and courteous. The police emergency number is 133. See **Crime & Theft**, **Emergency Numbers**.

Post Office: The head post office is to be found at Fleischmarkt 19 and is open 24 hr, as are the post offices at Westbahnhof and Südbahnhof and the central telegraph office of the Borseplatz. Sub-post offices usually open 0800-1800 Mon.-Fri. Queues can be long so make the most of the stamp vending machines situated outside most offices (postcards and letters under 20g to Europe 5 Sch, USA and Canada 11 Sch). Stamps can be bought at *Tabak-Trafik* and at most shops selling post cards. The address for the poste restante service is Hauptpostlagernd, Fleischmarkt 19, 1010 Vienna, and you will need your passport to collect any mail. See **Telephones & Telegrams**.

Prater: Originally the personal hunting grounds of Maximilian II and opened to the general public in 1766 by Joseph II. Today it represents the major recreation ground of the Viennese and is considered to be the birthplace of the Viennese Waltz, first heard here in 1820 with a composition by Strauss the Elder (see **A-Z**). See **PARKS & GARDENS**.

Public Holidays: 1 Jan. (New Year's Day); 6 Jan. (Epiphany); Good

Friday; Easter Monday; 1 May (Labour Day); Ascension; Whit Monday; Corpus Christi; 15 Aug. (Assumption); 26 Oct. (National Day); 1 Nov. (All Saints' Day); 8 Dec. (Immaculate Conception); 25, 26 Dec. (Christmas).

Rabies: Rabies still exists here as in other parts of the Continent. All animal bites should be seen to by a doctor and, if possible, you should get the name and address of the animal's owner. See **Health**.

Railways: There are two main stations in Vienna – the Westbahnhof, serving destinations in West Austria, Germany, France and Switzerland, and the Südbahnhof, serving Austria, Yugoslavia, Hungary and Italy. Both have Tourist Offices dealing with hotel reservations within Vienna and general travel throughout Austria. A third station, Franz-Josefs-Bahnhof, serves North Austria and Czechoslovakia. There are several formulae for cheap travel through Austria by rail apart from the usual Eurorail deals. The most advantageous is perhaps the *Puzzle Pass* under which the whole of Austria has been divided into several zones. When you buy the pass you specify how many zones you would like to cover. At 100 Sch per zone (minium three, maximum six) you have unlimited

train travel within the specified zones for a period of ten days. There is also the *Rabbit Card* giving reductions of up to 50%, the *Kilometrebank* (30%) or a yearly pass costing 990 Sch and allowing a reduction of 50% on each ticket. For further details contact the Tourist Offices in the stations mentioned above. See **Transport**.

Rathaus, Altes: See BUILDINGS 2.

Rathaus, Neues: See BUILDINGS 2.

Religious Services: For Catholics there is no shortage of churches where you can hear Mass; ask at the Tourist Office (see **Tourist Information**) for a list of churches where Mass is said in Latin and information on where to go for confessions or advice in English. There is one English-speaking Catholic church in Vienna at Boltzmanngasse 7. (1845 Sat., 1100 Sun.). Other religious denominations with services in English are:
Anglican – Jauresgasse 17-19. Info. Church Office (British Embassy).
Baptist – Mollardgasse 35. (Tel: 0223-13125). 0930, 1130 Sun.
Community Church – Dorotheergasse 16. 1130 Sun.

International Chapel – Bujattigasse 5. 1500 Sun.
Methodist – Sechshauser Strasse 56. 0915, 1100 Sun.
For the Jewish Community the City Temple is situated at
Seitenstettengasse 4, and information about prayer times can be
obtained from the Israelitische Kultusgemeinde, tel: 53104.

Riesenrad: Situated in the Prater (see **PARKS & GARDENS**, **A–Z**), this
giant Ferris wheel (54 m in diameter) was built in 1896 by the engineer
Walter B. Basset. It is an important Viennese landmark and featured in
the 1949 film *The Third Man*.

Ruprechtskirche: Built on the site of a Roman shrine (some stones
of which are thought to make up the present church), St. Ruprecht's is
the oldest church in Vienna. It dates back to AD 740 although most of
the present structure is Romanesque and Gothic. Note the fine stained
glass and the altar of Our Lady of Loretto, the Black Madonna, whose
help was invoked in times of danger. See **CHURCHES**, **WALK 1**.

Sailing: There are several sailing schools on the Alte Donau (Old Danube) that rent out boats and give lessons. English is usually spoken. Prices vary. For information, contact: Segelschule Hofbauer 22, An Der Ob Alte Donau 185, tel: 236733. U Alte Donau.

Schatzkammer: See MUSEUMS 1, Hofburg.

Schiele, Egon (1890-1918): Schiele was an expressionist painter whose work was influenced by Art Nouveau and by Freudian psychology. He is best known for his drawings of nudes, for which he was imprisoned briefly in 1912 on a charge of 'corrupting public morals'. Among his paintings which can be seen in various galleries are *Death and the Maiden*, *Windowscape* and *Woman with Two Children*. He died of influenza just as his talent was becoming recognized.

Schönbrunn Palace: The summer residence of the Hapsburgs was originally supposed to surpass Versailles in size and splendour but the budget did not stretch that far. The palace nevertheless contains 1441 rooms and was added onto by various members of the family down the generations. Franz I built the zoo in 1752 (see **CHILDREN**) and Maria Theresa added the Gloriette (see **A-Z**), the palace theatre and the pseudo Roman ruins. She was also responsible for the rococo style of the palace as it is today. Mozart (see **A-Z**) performed in the palace's Hall of Mirrors for Maria Theresa at the age of six. Napoleon resided here from 1805 to 1809 and his son died in the palace at the age of 21 after having been kept virtually a prisoner there by his father. Emperor Franz Joseph was born (1848) and died (1916) here and was the last Hapsburg to reside in Schönbrunn. It was also the site of the signing of the abdication of Karl I on 11 November 1918.
A tour of the State apartments will take you round the private rooms of Franz Joseph and Elizabeth but of particular interest is the 'Room of Mirrors', considered to be the ultimate in rococo style in the world, and decorated with 260 Indian miniatures.
The park is of formal design and contains some attractive fountains, for example the Schoner Brunnen to the left as you pass through the central arch and the Neptune Fountain (1780) straight ahead. If you walk

to the other side of the park you will come to a rise which is crowned with the Gloriette (see **A-Z**) which offers marvellous views of the castle and Wienerwald (Vienna Woods). See **BUILDINGS 1**, **PARKS & GARDENS**.

Schottenkirche: Built by Irish Benedicitine monks who were invited over to Vienna by the Babenburg ruler, Heinrich, in the 12thC. The name comes from the fact that Ireland was referred to as 'New Scotland' at the time. There is a fine baroque memorial by J. E. Fischer von Erlach to Graf von Starhemberg who defended Vienna against the Turks. There are also some interesting paintings of medieval Vienna in the abbey. See **CHURCHES**, **WALK 2**.

Schubert, Franz (1797-1828): Born in Vienna, he was a pupil of Salieri's. His earliest surviving works date from 1810, and his prolific output includes over 600 songs, four operas, chamber music, the 'Unfinished Symphony', the 'Great' C-major symphony, and the *Trout* piano quintet. His work brought him little financial reward and his survival as an independent composer was largely due to generous friends. He died of typhus at the age of 31.

Schubert Museum: See **MUSEUMS 2**.

Secession: The name given to a group of artists, the most notable being Gustav Klimt (see **A-Z**) and Oskar Kokoschka (1886-1980), who broke away from the Viennese art establishment in 1897 to form an autonomous movement. They exhibited their works in the 'Secession' building designed in *Jugendstil* style (Viennese Art Nouveau) by Joseph Maria Olbrich in 1899. See **WALK 4**.

Shopping: The most popular tourist shopping streets in Vienna are concentrated in the first district from the Opera House along Kärntner Strasse up to Stephansplatz, down Graben and left along Kohlmarkt. Rotenturmstrasse (from Stephansdom – see **A-Z** – down to the canal) is also worth exploring as are the numerous little adjoining streets. For more down-to-earth shopping – department stores, hi-fi equipment, sports and food – try the Mariahilferstrasse (between the Westbahnhof and the Messepalast). For antiques the best value is at the auction house, Dorotheum (see **SHOPPING 2**). See **SHOPPING 1 & 2**, **Best Buys**.

Sigmund Freud Museum: See MUSEUMS 2.

Smoking: Packets of cigarettes cost between 25 and 35 Sch from *Tabak-Trafik*, cafés, restaurants, etc. Austrian brands are towards the lower end of the price range and are generally of a good quality. Smoking is not allowed on public transport, in cinemas or public places but it is not considered to be a particularly antisocial habit.

Spanish Riding School: Since 1894 the magnificent room in the Winterreitschule (see **Hofburg**) has been used exclusively for the training of the white Lippizaner horses in their perfect displays of equestrian *haute école*. The Lippizaner stem from a Spanish breed and are named after the stud established in Lipic (in what is now Yugoslavia). They are born dark and usually turn white between their seventh and tenth year. Their training takes about four years and only the stallions are used. The main stud is now at Piber in Styria and the mares are kept here. In summer the stallions go there for a well-earned rest. See **CHILDREN**.

St. Marxer Friedhof: Leberstrasse 6-8. 0700-1800 April-Oct. Tram 71. This cemetery was used until the mid 1800s, and it is here that Mozart (see **A-Z**) was buried in 1791.

Staatsoper: Operas were first performed in Vienna in 1688 on the site of the National Library, then in the old Burgtheater, then the Kärntnertor Theatre and following that, in the Ring Theater which was destroyed by fire, before moving into the Opera House on its completion in 1869. It opened with Mozart's *Don Giovanni*. The building was bombed in March 1945 and completely gutted by fire after which reconstruction was not completed until 1955 when it reopened with Beethoven's *Fidelio*.
A tour of the interior will reveal a surprisingly modest although elegant auditorium which, together with the stage, is the scene of the famous Opera Ball. See **BUILDINGS 2**, **WALK 3**, **Opera**.

Stephansdom: The cathedral is situated in the heart of Vienna with all 23 of the city's districts encircling it. It was begun in the 12thC and has since been continually worked on and today represents architectural developments through eight centuries. It sustained extensive damage during World War II when the great Pummerin bell (founded in 1711 from Turkish cannonballs) fell and shattered. The pieces were recovered and melted down to be recast. You can take a lift up to see the bell (0900-1730 daily). The climb of 312 steps up the south tower which dominates the skyline will reward you with a wonderful view over the city. One of the most striking features inside the cathedral is the 16thC pulpit sculpted by Anton Pilgram which depicts the heads of the Fathers of the Church – Augustine, Gregory, Ambrose and Jerome – in fine detail. The high altar (1647) is in baroque style and a sombre work in black marble. To the left is the Virgin's Choir (Marienchor) with a splendid Gothic altarpiece, the Wiener Neustadt (1884), and, containing the tomb of the founder of the cathedral, Rudolph IV. On the other side of the high altar is the Apostle's Choir (Apostelchor) with the magnificent tomb of Frederick II, the work of Nikolaus of Leydon (1467-1513). There are tours of the maze-like catacombs beneath the structure in which there is a crypt containing the bones of countless plague victims, the Hapsburgs internal organs (minus hearts) and the remains of the basilica that originally stood on this site (tours 1000-1130, 1400-1630 daily). See **CHURCHES, WALK 1**.

Stephansplatz: The heart of the city and site of St. Stephen's Cathedral. Considerably damaged in the war, the area was laid out as a pedestrian zone directly on top of the underground station. It was somewhat spoilt by the lack of attention given to conserving the architectural integrity of the area although the controversial modern glass building on the corner is an improvement. Under the square lies the Virgil Kapelle which was discovered, along with Roman remains, when digging the subway. The outline of the chapel is marked in coloured stones. You can visit it via the underground station (1000-1600

Tue.-Fri., 1400-1800 Sat., 0900-1300 Sun. & hol.).

Stock-im-Eisen: A tree trunk into which many nails have been hammered for good luck by journeymen blacksmiths. It stands at the junction of Graben (see **A-Z**) and Kärntner Strasse (see **A-Z**). See **WALK 1**.

Strauss, Johann the Elder (1804-49): Strauss was musical director of the Zum Sperl, a place of entertainment, by his mid 20s. Before he was 30 he was taking his 28-strong orchestra on highly successful European tours such as the one in 1838 to Buckingham Palace for Queen Victoria's coronation. In 1846 he received an appointment to the Viennese court. He composed countless waltzes, quadrilles, polkas and marches, the most famous being the *Radetzky March*.

Strauss, Johann the Younger (1825-99): More successful than his father, Strauss the Younger made his debut with his own orchestra when he was only 19, then toured Europe and the USA as the 'Waltz King'. His most famous composition is the *Blue Danube*, but he also composed popular operettas including *Die Fledermaus* (1874) and *The Gypsy Baron* (1885).

Students: Vienna is not a cheap city to visit but certain reductions are available to students. To benefit from these you will need an International Student Identity Card (ISIC) which you should get before leaving home. You will be asked to show it for any reduced-price ticket, e.g. at the railway station, or for cheap theatre tickets (nearly all offer a 20% student reduction). For full details and general student advice apply to:
Zentralausschuss, Liechtensteinstrasse 13, tel: 346518/346519.
Int Studentenclub, Schottengasse 1, tel: 634582.
WUK., Wahringerstrasse 59, tel: 438220.
For a cheap and friendly café where you can

meet other students, try: Studentencafe, Berggasse 5, tel: 316508. See
Youth Hostels.

Taxis: There are numerous taxi stands. Taxis can also be hailed in the
street or you can call one by phone (tel: 4369/3130). The pick-up
charge is 22 Sch and then 10 Sch per km. If you phone for a taxi there
is a supplementary charge of 10 Sch. If you have a complaint, ask for a
receipt, take the driver's number and contact the company.

Telephones & Telegrams: There are numerous telephone cabins
around the city that take 1, 5 and 10 Sch coins or a telephone card.
The latter (*Wertkarte*) are available from *Tabak-Trafik*, the post office or
automatic machines (you will need five 10 Sch coins). They are worth
buying if you have a lot of calls to make especially as some hotels add
a 200% charge when you phone from your room. National and international calls are cheaper 1800-0800 Mon.-Fri. and all day at weekends and on public holidays. Direct dialling is nearly always possible
but if you need help dial 16 for Directory Enquiries (Austria), 08 for
international dialling codes and 09 for the International Operator.
NB: The whole of the telephone network is currently being revised and
telephone numbers change all the time. If you have any problems call
Directory Enquiries.
Telegrams must contain more than seven words and can be sent from
post offices (see **A-Z**) or by phone. The central telegram office is at
Borseplatz 1 and is open 24 hours. Letter-telegrams cost half the price
of an ordinary telegram and the procedure is the same except that they
are delivered with the ordinary post (minimum of 22 words).

Television & Radio: There are two state television channels (foreign films are always dubbed) as well as cable TV. Radio Blue Danube
broadcasts in English, French and Spanish throughout Austria.

Time Difference: One hour ahead of GMT. The clocks are put for-
ward one hour in the summer (April-Sep.)

Tipping: As a general rule 10% is the accepted tip for taxi drivers, waiters and tourist guides. In a hairdresser leave 20-30 Sch. Porters expect at least 5 Sch per bag and chambermaids about 50 Sch for long stays. You are not obliged to tip in the toilets if you have to pay for the use of them but otherwise leave a few Schillings for the attendant.

Toilets: Public toilets in Vienna are extremely clean. They are often located in underground stations or parks, and you will have to pay about 5 Sch. Other than that you can use the toilets of a coffee house (customers only) or a museum.

Tourist Information: The central Tourist Office for information about Vienna is situated at Kärnter Strasse 38 (tel: 5138892) and is open daily from 0900-1900. They have a wide choice of useful pamphlets and a good city map as well as piles of free events-listings magazines. There are also branches at the airport (see **A-Z**) and railway stations (see **Railways**). For information about the rest of Austria go to Margaretenstrasse 1 (tel: 5872000) which is open 0900-1730 Mon.-Fri. If you want information specifically on Lower Austria you should go to Heidenschusse 2 (tel: 5333114) 0900-1700 Mon.-Fri. The address of the Vienna Tourist Board is A-1095 Vienna Kinderspitalgasse 5 (not open to the public) and this is where you should write with any complaints (see **A-Z**). For an 'off the beaten track' guided walk through the city ask for the *Vienna Guides* pamphlet at the Tourist Offices. In it you will find descriptions and details of the walks they offer. You simply turn up at the appointed time. Walks of about 1hr 30 min cost 95 Sch per adult, 70 Sch for students and are free for those under 15 years. For details of their museum visits, topical tours or coach tours contact Brigitte Timmermann at 69/1 Wiethestrasse, A-1220 Vienna, tel: 2202620.

Trams: A fun, convenient and ecologically friendly way to visit Vienna, the trams have a better-developed network than the underground and are easier to use than the buses. To gain access or alight, press the button next to one of the several doors along the length of the tram. A recorded message announces each stop and which buses, trams or underground you can change onto. See **Transport**.

Transport: Public transport in Vienna is reliable, clean and easy to use rendering the private car redundant. It consists of trams, buses and an underground network and provides access to all of Vienna's tourist attractions. There are information centres manned by friendly, English-speaking staff at the following underground stations: Karlsplatz (Opern Passage) – tel: 5873186; Stephansplatz – tel: 5124227; Praterstern – tel: 249302; Philadelphiabrücke – tel: 8138401. For a clear idea of the network you can buy a detailed map at the information centres for 10 Sch. The city is divided into several transport zones but as the first zone extends out to Schönbrunn Palace (see **BUILDINGS 1**, **A–Z**), it is the only one that concerns most visitors. Several passes exist which enable you to use any of the services and can be bought at a *Tabak-Trafik* or travel agency. The most useful are the *24 Hours Vienna* or *72 Hours Vienna* costing 40 and 102 Sch respectively. Once the pass is cancelled by punching it in the ticket machine the first time you use it, you can travel for 24 (or 72) hours on the bus, tram or underground in the first zone. Alternatively, coupon tickets for four or eight rides (or one ride in four or eight zones) can be bought for 56 or 112 Sch. Bend the card back to punch the correct part each time you use it. Single tickets cost 20 Sch each (you will need two 10 Sch coins). Children under six years do not pay and those up to 15 years can obtain a half-fare pass for 7 Sch. See **Buses**, **Railways**, **Trams**, **Underground**.

Traveller's Cheques: See **Money**.

Uhrenmuseum der Stadt Wien: See MUSEUMS 1.

Underground: Although not fully developed as yet, the underground is easy to use and the quickest way to travel within Vienna. The fare structure is the same as for the buses and trams. There are currently three main underground lines (blue numbers preceded by a 'U' on the maps) – U1 running from Zentrum Kagran in the northeast to Reumann in the south; U2 running along the Ring from Schottenring to Karlsplatz; and U4 from Hutteldorf-Hacking in the west, past Schönbrunn Palace (see **BUILDINGS 1**, **A–Z**), looping round the centre to finish at Heiligenstadt to the northwest. They all go through Karlsplatz

(see **A-Z**). U6 serving the Westbahnhof on a vertical axis was recently opened, and plans are underway for U3 to run across the old part of Vienna and out to the east. See **Transport**.

Vienna Boys' Choir: The boys are chosen for the pure quality of their voices and, as well as being trained in singing, are also given a formal education at the school of the Choir in the Augarten Palace. When their voices break they join the Chor Viennese but after leaving school are free to take up professions that are unrelated to music. Nowadays there are four choirs, each of 24 boys, who take turns singing at the Burgkapelle (see **Hofburg**).

Volksgarten: See PARKS & GARDENS.

Waffensammlung: See MUSEUMS 1.

What's On: The best Austrian publication for news of what's happening in Vienna is the weekly *Falter* magazine, available in all newsagents. They also publish a very good annual guide to restaurants, bars and discos called *Wien Wie es Ist*. The Tourist Office produces some excellent English guides to events These include the biannual publication *Scene* (winter or summer) and the annual *Coming Events*. Both can be obtained free from the Austrian Tourist Office in London. They also publish *Termine* monthly which is in German. See **Tourist Information**.

Youth Hostels: The addresses of the two most centrally placed youth hostels are:
Myrthengasse 7 (7th District), tel: 936396.
Friedrich-Engels-Platz 24 (20th District), tel: 3382940.
You will need an International Youth Hostel Federation card which you should obtain before leaving the UK and it is advisable to book in advance. Expect to pay around 130 Sch per night with breakfast and 50 Sch per meal. A full list of the various Youth Hostels within the Vienna region is available from the Tourist Office (see **A-Z**).

Zentralfriedhof: Simmering Hauptstrasse 234. 0800-1700 (winter), 0700-1900 (summer). Tram 71. This is the largest cemetery in Austria and was first opened in 1872. Here are the graves of the famous composers, writers and artists such as Beethoven (see **A-Z**), Strauss Jr (see **A-Z**), Schubert (see **A-Z**), Brahms (see **A-Z**), Salieri, Kraus, Nestroy and Schnitzler, to name but a few. A map is available at the main gate.